REWARDS OF

*Also by Ivor Gurney
from MidNAG/Carcanet*

Collected Letters

Severn & Somme/War's Embers

War Letters

Best Poems/The Book of Five Makings

80 Poems or so

IVOR GURNEY

REWARDS OF WONDER
Poems of Cotswold, France, London

EDITED BY
GEORGE WALTER

Mid Northumberland Arts Group

Carcanet Press

2000

First published in 2000 by
Mid Northumberland Arts Group
Woodhorn Colliery Museum
Ashington
Northumberland NE63 9YS

in association with

Carcanet Press Limited
4th Floor, Conavon Court
12–16 Blackfriars Street
Manchester M3 5BQ

A CIP catalogue record for this book
is available from the British Library
ISBN 0 904790 90 8 (MidNAG)
ISBN 1 85754 424 2 (Carcanet)

The publishers acknowledge financial assistance
from the Arts Council of England and Northern Arts

Set in 10.5/12pt Ehrhardt by XL Publishing Services, Tiverton
Printed and bound in England by SRP Ltd, Exeter

Contents

Introduction	1
A Note on the Text	17
Acknowledgements	19
Rewards of Wonder:	
Poems of Cotswold, France, London	21
Textual Notes	103
Explanatory Notes	125
Maps	143
Chronology	146
Texts Cited and Further Reading	159
Index of Titles and First Lines	161

Introduction

Over the years, various euphemisms have been used to refer to Ivor Gurney's mental illness. His contemporaries spoke discreetly of 'the cloud coming over him' or his being 'lost to the world', whilst later commentators prefer to talk more precisely of his 'ill-health', his 'over-delicate sensibility' or his 'depression'. Whether discreet or precise, these euphemisms have all had the effect of glossing over the disturbing reality of Gurney's condition, making him seem instead like the kind of sensitive genius who exemplifies Dryden's famous remark that 'Great wits are sure to madness near allied / And thin partitions do their bounds divide'. Implicit in this romantic perception of genius is the notion that such personalities are always doomed to tragedy and that, sooner or later, insanity ceases to be the midwife of creativity and becomes instead a source of terrible affliction. In Gurney's case, there seems little point in trying to separate his talent from his illness or his illness from his destiny: according to Edmund Blunden, all three are a reflection of 'the merciless intensity of his spirit' (Blunden 1954: 19).

Gurney's tragic potential is also heightened by historical circumstances. It comes as no surprise to read that his experiences on the Western Front between 1916 and 1917 not only resulted in his being discharged from the army with shell-shock, but also 'contributed to the final breakdown of the balance of his mind' (Stephen 1988: 337). If any explanation needs to be found for Gurney's insanity, what better place to look than amidst the bloodshed and waste of the trenches? Fifteen months' active service in such horrific circumstances would leave its mark on even the strongest temperament and Gurney was, of course, a creative artist; little wonder then that the war made him 'one of its embers, ruined forever by its fires' (Clark 1973: 31). Some believed that this devastation left Gurney 'unable to write anything, whilst always haunted by the sense that it was all there waiting to be grasped' (anon 1937b: 14); others preferred to picture him rendered 'unable to distinguish the past from the present . . . writing war poetry as though the war was still on'

(Black 1970: 145). Either way, the image of Gurney as an ill-starred genius whose talent was destroyed in the killing fields of France persisted.

The tremendous revival of interest in Gurney's life and work over the past two decades has led to the emergence of a more accurate picture of his mental illness. His biographer Michael Hurd was the first to suggest that to cast him in the role of 'war victim' was 'simplistic and sentimental' and that the real source of his insanity was 'buried deeper and more fundamentally in Gurney's own nature' (Hurd 1978: 195). Hurd's diagnosis of paranoid schizophrenia was supported by Sir William Trethowan's extensive research into Gurney's condition and, more recently, by Gordon Claridge's work on the psychopathology of creativity. Measuring Gurney's symptoms against the twelve operational criteria used in version 3.3. of the OPCRIT diagnostic system, Claridge found that eleven gave a diagnosis of schizophrenia, whilst the twelfth – the Research Diagnostic Criteria – classified his illness as a bipolar schizoaffective disorder. Such agreement leaves little room for doubt that Gurney suffered from 'a long-standing illness of a severely schizophrenic type' (Claridge 1998: 242).

This surge of interest has also shed new light on the impact of Gurney's madness on his ability to work effectively. Far from silencing him, his insanity seems to have been the catalyst for a phenomenal outburst of creative energy. Confined within the walls of the City of London Mental Hospital at Dartford, he wrote more than ever – indeed, over half of his surviving autograph poems and a third of his surviving songs were produced after his arrival there. Moreover, to suggest that he was labouring under the illusion that the Great War was still underway whilst writing this material is to ignore one of the most curious features of his particular type of psychotic illness. What marks out schizophrenia from other functional and organic mental disorders is the way in which sufferers from the disease manage to keep a firm hold on everyday reality; they know 'what day and year it is, can read the newspaper, recognise friends and relatives and converse intelligently' (Gottesman 1991: 22). Gurney may have been deluded, but those delusions did not prevent him from being fully aware of his immediate surroundings or the circumstances in which he found himself.

Nevertheless, much more still remains to be done before the precise relationship between Gurney's illness and his creativity can be fully understood. Whilst his incarceration is no longer talked of as 'the damning blow' which ended his career (anon 1937a: 1), it is still seen as marking a turning-point in his development as an artist. This applies less to his song-writing activities because so few of his later settings have actually made their way into print; as Hurd notes, the publication of this material 'requires radical editorial interference – with all the moral and ethical considerations that raises' (Hurd *et al.* 1998: 3). His poetry, on the other hand, is now conveniently categorised as either 'pre-asylum' or 'asylum', a distinction which is used to refer both to *when* it was written and also to *how* it is written. Dividing up his poetic output in this way implies not only that his 'sane' work bears little relation to his 'mad' work, but also that the innovative nature of his later writing owes more to his schizophrenia than to any calculated effort on his part. Gurney's poetry, the argument goes, is distinctive and challenging not because he strove to make it so but because by 'throwing off sanity, he also threw off the shackles of contemporary poetry and proceeded to become a remarkable poet' (Taylor 1987: 103).

There is, however, one collection of poems in the Gurney Archive which cannot be comfortably classified as either pre-asylum or asylum. Begun almost twelve months before Gurney was finally certified insane and completed three years later when he was profoundly psychotic, *Rewards of Wonder* transcends the chronological constraints usually imposed upon his poetry and offers powerful evidence of the continuities which exist between his earlier and later work. It also throws fresh light upon how Gurney's schizophrenia affected his creative practices and provides a rare insight into his activities as a textual producer, most notably the amount of painstaking labour that went into his conscious search for the most appropriate poetic idiom. Ranging over the subjects that inspire his best work – his home county, real and imagined Londons and, for the first time since the Armistice, his experiences on the Western Front – *Rewards of Wonder* shows Gurney mastering his insanity and using it to create a wholly different kind of poetry, making it a remarkable collection in its own right and a crucial addition to the Gurney canon.

A History of Rewards of Wonder

By September 1921, Gurney had finally given up all pretence of being a student at the Royal College of Music and returned to Gloucestershire. Moving in with his aunt in Longford, he tried to support himself by taking a succession of menial labouring jobs but soon found that he was both physically and mentally unsuited to this kind of manual drudgery. He was still frantically writing, producing what he described to his friend and mentor Marion Scott as 'feeble songs' (Thornton 1991: 522) whilst simultaneously drafting and revising new poems in a school exercise book, on long sheets of loose lined paper and in two hardcover notebooks, one bound in black and the other in green. Two short-lived posts as a cinema pianist in Bude and Plumstead over Christmas and the New Year did not hinder his progress and, by January 1922, he had also begun to fill a new pink marbled hard-cover exercise book with revisions of earlier material and yet more new poems.

Back in Longford, Gurney made the decision to submit a new collection of poetry to Sidgwick & Jackson. Rather than draw on his most recent work, he instead spent March and April trawling through older manuscripts in search of material that would more fully represent his development as a poet over the past three years. His final choice of '80 poems or so' were typed up by his sister Dorothy and hastily despatched to his publishers. They were swiftly rejected on the grounds that they looked 'more like a poet's notebook than a volume of finished poems'. Undaunted, he made radical revisions to the typescript, reducing it to half of its original length and correcting those texts which remained, and resubmitted it as 'Forty Poems' in the second week of June. When this amended version was also politely refused by Frank Sidgwick, Gurney passed on the typescripts firstly to Lascelles Abercrombie and then to Edmund Blunden for a second opinion (Walter & Thornton 1997: 4-5, 9).

Gurney's correspondence with Abercrombie has not survived, but it is clear from the tone of his letters to Blunden that he was growing increasingly desperate, describing himself in one as 'an unsuccessful and angry poet writing to a successful poet who has already done things for him' (Thornton 1991: 539). Efforts made on his behalf by Walter de la Mare and Sir Edward Marsh had provided him with a job at Gloucester Tax Office, but his rapidly deteriorating mental state meant that he was unable to keep it for long. Moving in uninvited with his brother Ronald and his new wife, he made repeated suicide attempts, believing that 'electrical tricks' were being played on him. In September 1922, in a final attempt to see his work in print, he forwarded his sister's typescript and the black, green and pink marbled hard-cover exercise books to Marsh, apologising for 'the horrible state of some of it' but explaining that he was 'pretty badly done nowadays' (Thornton 1991: 524). Shortly afterwards, he was certified insane by two local doctors and admitted to Barnwood House, a private asylum just outside Gloucester. At the end of the year, he was transferred to the City of London Mental Hospital at Dartford, where he remained for the rest of his life.

At some point after Gurney's committal, Marion Scott managed to retrieve the three hardcover exercise books from Marsh and either arranged to have them typed or typed them out herself. Gurney's disturbed mental condition after his move to Dartford seems to have interrupted his creative activities during the early months of 1923, but by May he had received carbon-copies of the poems in the pink and green notebooks and made extensive revisions to them. He returned them to Marion Scott on 'a day of agony', proudly telling her that 'The verses are all corrected. The scraps are made long – and many made longer' (Gurney 10.47); she then passed them on to J. C. Squire, the editor of the *London Mercury*. He chose fourteen poems from the mass of typescripts and printed them in his journal over the next decade in an attempt to keep Gurney's name in the public eye. Sadly, the only responses he seems to have received were 'letters of abuse' demanding to know why he had published such 'incoherent' texts (Gurney 5.12.2).

By July 1924, Gurney had selected a hundred of the same carbon-copies, arranged them as a unified volume and given it the title of

'Rewards of Wonder'. This he passed on to Marion Scott for retyping and, towards the end of the month, a payment of £1.5s was made to 'Miss Molly Hart, for typing Gurney's poems' (Gurney 11.1.2). This is presumably the version of *Rewards of Wonder* to which Gurney was referring when he wrote to Sir Robert Baden Powell in August, describing himself as 'first war poet of England – Musician – Poet – scholar of all sorts of high rank' and appealing for '7 books of verse' to be published (Gurney 52.11.141). Only 'Rewards of wonder' and 'Day spaces and Makings' are mentioned by name in this letter, but fortunately an appeal addressed to Sir Edward Marsh written at the same time supplies the titles of the remaining five: 'Ridge Clay, Limestone', 'La Flandre, and By Norton', 'Roman gone East', 'London seen Clear' and 'Fatigues and Magnificences' (Gurney 52.11.137). Of these, only *Rewards of Wonder* is still extant.

At the same time as he was pleading for its publication, Gurney was also making extensive revisions to the Hart typescript, adding a whole new poem called 'What I Will Pay' from the green exercise book carbon-copies and expanding the collection's title to include the phrase 'Poems of Cotswold, France, London'. These revisions were evidently finished by 18 October 1924, as a letter to Marion Scott postmarked with this date shows. In it, Gurney informed her that the typescript had been sent to 'Sir R Forbes Roberts – from whom I have had wireless of praise' (Gurney 10.38). Gurney's medical records show that one of the main symptoms of his illness was a belief that messages were being passed on to him through the radio, suggesting that the 'praise' he felt was forthcoming was most likely imaginary. It is thus impossible to say whether or not Forbes Roberts ever actually saw the revised Hart typescript; the likelihood is that it was retrieved by a member of the hospital's staff and passed on to Marion Scott for safe keeping.

If *Rewards of Wonder* was in her possession from this point onwards, it would help to explain the extensive alterations made by Gurney to the green hardback notebook in February 1925; wishing to work on *Rewards of Wonder* but finding himself without a copy, he would have had to have been content with correcting these earlier drafts instead. Even if Miss Scott had failed to take possession of it earlier, the revised

Hart typescript was certainly available to her three years later. In February 1928, Victor Gollancz expressed an interest in publishing a new collection of Gurney's poetry, and it was Marion Scott who undertook the task of making a representative selection. Her final choice of thirty-nine poems included fifteen from *Rewards of Wonder* and was given to Mollie Hart for typing, but Gollancz's enthusiasm seems to have quickly waned and sadly the project went no further.

Fifteen years passed before a complete copy of *Rewards of Wonder* was finally made. Concerned that those of Gurney's poems which only existed as autograph manuscripts or corrected typescripts might be lost in wartime, his old teacher Ralph Vaughan Williams paid 'a very good typist in Dorking' to make duplicates of them in September 1943 (Gurney 51.4). She did a thorough job, transcribing not only the final version of *Rewards of Wonder* but also six other Dartford collections and three hundred-odd loose manuscript poems. In addition, the pink marbled notebook typescripts altered by Gurney in 1923 but never used for *Rewards of Wonder* were also copied and gathered together under the title *Poems by Ivor Gurney (The Marbled Book, with later Additions)*.

By the time Edmund Blunden embarked on his pioneering edition of Gurney's unpublished poems a decade later, the originals of most of the texts that Vaughan Williams had arranged to have copied had disappeared. Blunden was thus forced to rely almost solely on Vaughan Williams's transcriptions for copy-text, but his practice of removing the poems he required from these typescript sets and not returning them afterwards meant the loss of more important primary material. Thankfully, the Gurney Archive in Gloucester Library was established in 1959 in an attempt to preserve what remained of Gurney's work and it was here that the Vaughan Williams typescript of *Rewards of Wonder* came to rest in the early 1960s. Today, it is catalogued as item Gurney 16 in the Archive's extensive holdings.

The Language of Schizophrenia
Despite the absence of so many pieces of this textual jigsaw, it is still possible to map most of the corrections that Gurney made to *Rewards of Wonder* during his first two years in the City of London Mental

Hospital. A comparison of the pink and green manuscript notebooks with J.C. Squire's *London Mercury* texts and what remains of the Vaughan Williams typescript shows him making two sorts of revisions, frequently amending both the punctuation and the wording of a text whilst almost always extending the whole text by adding extra lines of verse after the poem's original ending. Usually, this is limited to two or three additional lines, but a significant number of poems – 'Late May', for example, or 'Billet' – are almost doubled in length. Related examples of this tendency are the way in which 'Riez Bailleul' and 'Riez Bailleul Also' start out as a single twenty-five line poem in the pink manuscript notebook, only to become two separate poems of twenty-five and ten lines respectively by the time *Rewards of Wonder* is finally completed.

These corrections should in theory reflect the rapid deterioration in Gurney's mental state after his committal. Bent Rosenbaum and Harly Sonne, in their analysis of the linguistic features of schizophrenic writing, found that texts produced by actively psychotic individuals always displayed profound failure of deixis – in other words, an inability to maintain the system of anchoring and reference that ensures that a piece of writing remains intelligible (Rosenbaum & Sonne 1986: 45). Not surprisingly, there are myriad examples of this kind of incoherence amongst Gurney's Dartford papers; take, for example, his letter to Sir Robert Baden Powell appealing for the publication of *Rewards of Wonder*:

> Humbly asking Sir R. Baden Powell to do something for me – whether for crucifixion or free life. Or to do something which shall compel the granting of free leave of crucifixion. (absolutely effectual) My God, my God, they torture so. As to oaths of Death I have broken more Was knocked off two. (1) promised – electrically. (2) Electrical prevention. Shocks unbearable – an oath dissolved that directly I was free I would go and see the Monument police and take judgement.

The thematic confusion, the collapsing grammar, the absence of a structured narrative – all these indicate that Gurney was in a state of active psychosis when he made this appeal.

There is, however, no trace of this failure of deixis in *Rewards of Wonder* itself. The revisions made by Gurney after his committal are entirely congruous with his original texts: there are *no* obvious thematic, syntactical or grammatical differences between the material which he completed between 1921 and 1922 and the additions which he made in 1923 and 1924. More interestingly, only three out of the hundred and two poems in the collection show any trace of the kind of psychotic rhetoric that characterises his letters of appeal. But 'Today', 'Poets' and 'Strange Hells' are all substantially complete in their manuscript versions, suggesting that the references they contain to 'unclean hells' and 'tortures beyond men' are not so much indications of delusional thinking but merely elements of a broader poetic discourse entirely under Gurney's control. In short, as strange as it may seem, *Rewards of Wonder* appears to be free of any trace of its author's schizophrenia.

One way to explain this unexpected state of affairs would be to argue that Gurney only worked on *Rewards of Wonder* during those periods of temporary remission experienced by all schizophrenics – in other words, that his revisions are evidence of some kind of abiding sanity during the early years of his incarceration. But Gurney's medical records fail to support this idea: they state that he was 'highly depressed and agitated' during his first two years at Dartford, aside from a brief period in March 1924 when he became 'worse mentally and very threatening at times'. Indeed, the only significant improvement in his condition came in March 1925 and coincided with the appointment of Dr Randolph Davis as Second Assistant Medical Officer at the hospital. Davis's presence may have had a significant effect on Gurney's mental state, but he was soon dismissed from his post and plans for him to take Gurney as a private patient were aborted when it emerged that Davis was 'a charlatan, deep in debt, and eager only for the down-payment that would stave off his creditors' (Hurd 1978: 163).

The real answer seems to lie in the precise nature of Gurney's insanity. It was noted earlier that schizophrenics retain control of certain cognitive functions even when profoundly ill; in Gurney's case, these functions seem inextricably linked with his creativity. Dr

E.W. Anderson, Second Assistant Medical Officer at Dartford between 1925 and 1929, noted that Gurney could appear quite rational when 'induced to talk about music or poetry' (Trethowan 1981: 304) and it could be argued that this normal functioning also came into play when Gurney was actually writing poetry. Powerful evidence for this argument is offered by the research of Rhodes *et al.* into the relationship between psychosis and creativity. Attempting to explain why poems by some psychotics seem to differ so little from normal poetry, they draw on Jacobson's theory that language has a linguistically separate poetic function to argue that 'the poetic function of language is less impaired than other functions' in certain psychotic individuals (Rhodes *et al.* 1995: 318). Gurney, it would seem, was one of those individuals.

Further evidence points to the fact that the formal qualities of poetry can actually help schizophrenics control the severe auditory hallucinations which are a symptom of their illness. Daniel Paul Schreber, a contemporary of Gurney's afflicted with the same disease, found that three activities made 'even the most drawn-out voices perish': playing the piano, reading and especially the act of committing poems to memory (Peterson 1982: 159–60). According to his medical records, playing the piano and reading were Gurney's main activities during his first two years at Dartford. This information is hardly surprising given his musical and literary interests, but it takes on an added significance in the light of Schreber's experiences. And, of course, Gurney's interest in these areas also had a practical outlet: if Schreber found that reading poetry helped to alleviate his voices, surely Gurney would find a similar or even greater measure of relief through actually writing poetry.

Inscribing Madness in Rewards of Wonder

It must be remembered, however, that whilst *Rewards of Wonder* may fail to incorporate the more overt signs of Gurney's insanity, it is still a schizophrenic text. It certainly reveals traces of heightened significance, the process in schizoid thinking whereby a schizophrenic's attention becomes 'trapped on one topic or word, rather as happens when a record becomes cracked' (Howe 1991: 29); this particular word or idea assumes an unnatural significance for the sufferer, leaving them unable to move on to other subjects, and is endlessly repeated in their written and visual productions. In this case, the object of obsession is the text itself: the endless revision and rewriting of certain poems in *Rewards of Wonder* – 'Laventie', for example, or 'Thoughts of New England' – suggest that Gurney is truly unable to drag himself away from these poems and move on to producing new material. Even when he does finally leave a particular text alone, Gurney frequently reiterates its contents and themes in other poems with the same name – 'The Ford' and 'First Time In' spring to mind in this respect – making *Rewards of Wonder* sound at times indeed like the cracked record that Howe describes.

Heightened significance is also suggested by the way in which Gurney seems to lock on to certain key words or names in these texts. 'England', 'war', 'Rome', 'Gloucester' and 'poet' all appear with monotonous frequency, as do references to Gurney's 'right', his 'wonder' and his need for 'honour' in particular. Persons of significance for Gurney, such as Ben Jonson, are also regularly referred to, sometimes directly but also through a complex system of metonymic allusion: the phrase 'Forth going to sea' in 'New Year's Eve' relates to Jonson because of the time he spent at Hawthornden in the Firth of Forth, visiting his fellow poet William Drummond. 'Forth' also links Jonson directly to Drummond, which in turn links Gurney's 'Master' to both Annie Nelson Drummond, his lost Scottish love whom he nicknamed 'Hawthornden', and the Hawthornden Prize for Poetry which Gurney seems to have felt he should have won (Thornton 1991: 538).

The self-referential nature of this kind of punning also suggests another symptom of schizoid thinking. Known as 'blunted affect', it manifests itself through both 'a conspicuous incapacity for emotional empathy' (Gottesman 1991: 36) and an 'intense preoccupation with the self' (Claridge *et al.* 1990: 236). Gurney's allusions all work in this highly self-referential way; it is only possible for the reader to make sense of the multiple references to Ben Jonson if he or she is aware of Gurney's strong identification with Jonson, the reasons behind this identification – they both saw military service in Flanders, they both

have associations with Scotland and they both express a stubborn
belief in their own superior talent – and the fact that Jonson was thus
the most venerated of Gurney's 'Masters'. In effect, what Gurney
seems to be doing in *Rewards of Wonder* is moving towards a system of
reference which takes no account of anyone but himself; there appears
to be no sense of a potential audience, but rather a linguistic and
thematic self-referentiality that borders on the solipsistic.

Recognising the subtlety with which the symptoms of Gurney's
mental illness are inscribed in *Rewards of Wonder* means that it is
necessary to look again at the practice of categorising his poetry as
either 'pre-asylum' or 'asylum'. The use of these categories implies
that it is possible to draw a line between two distinct phases in
Gurney's development, one in which he was writing sanely and the
other in which he was writing whilst in the throes of madness. But
once it is acknowledged that those qualities that mark *Rewards of
Wonder* out as a schizophrenic text are present in all of Gurney's work
– Blunden saw them as giving Gurney's poetry its 'peculiar unconven-
tionality' and 'uncommon melody' (Blunden 1953: 19) – then that
distinction becomes meaningless. Everything that he wrote is charac-
terised by cognitive processes which, in their most overt forms, are
used to diagnose a recognised form of clinical insanity; how then is it
possible to make a distinction between those of his poems which
should be seen as 'sane' and those which should be seen as 'insane'?
Gurney's certification in September 1922 is certainly a key moment
biographically speaking, but the lifelong nature of his illness and the
enduring impact that it had upon his creativity means that regarding
his committal as some kind of turning-point in his artistic evolution
creates a highly artificial picture of that evolution.

'the wrought out links / Of fancy to fancy'
Viewed in this light, it would be easy to assume that Gurney's is a
distinctive voice in twentieth-century poetry not because he strove to
make it so, but because of his mental illness. Acknowledging the extent
to which his work is characterised by elements of schizophrenic
discourse seems to add weight to the image of him as some kind of
gifted amateur whose poetic achievement owes more to tragic

serendipity than any conscious effort on his part. Yet even the briefest glance at the complex textual history of *Rewards of Wonder* suggests that the opposite is true; the extensive reworking and reshaping that this collection underwent during the four years of its gestation shows Gurney to be a committed craftsman whose poetic effects are only achieved after a great deal of hard work. Time and time again he returns to individual poems, revising phrases or whole lines, deleting others and adding new material; he also makes considered choices as to what should appear in the completed volume, including multiple texts of some poems to show the kind of subtle differences in language and meaning that he can draw out from the same raw material. These are not the actions of a careless scribbler pouring out the first thing that comes into his head, but rather those of a skilful artist striving to create a wholly new kind of poetic utterance.

Indeed, it is precisely because Gurney was so aware of his illness – what he called his 'neurasthenia' (Thornton 1991: 32) – that he became such a craftsman. His pre-war interest in Müller's exercise system, his joining up in 1915 and his forays into the world of hard manual labour all reflect his belief that strict discipline would combat or at least control his schizophrenia (Thornton 1991: 10, 87, 481). Aware also of the damage that his illness might do to his writing if left unchecked, he attempted to exert a similar kind of discipline upon his creative practices. Many of his poems draw attention to the importance of craftsmanship as a way of imposing this discipline; allusions to squareness and order are everywhere in his post-war work, both as a counterbalance to what he calls 'the dark thoughts within' (Walter & Thornton 1997: 113) and also as a means by which those thoughts can be controlled and used productively. Recognising that 'virtue lies in a square making' (Walter & Thornton 1997: 120) is a recognition of the value of such squareness as a way of imposing order upon his burgeoning insanity. Elsewhere, he is more explicit about the need to impose order upon his mental processes: 'I musician have wrestled with the stuff in making, / And wrought a square thing out of my stubborn mind' (Kavanagh 1982: 119). When he announces that he writes 'to keep madness and black torture away' (Kavanagh 1982: 200), he is acknowledging not only the cathartic impulses that underlie his activities, but also his fight to eliminate the more overt signs of his illness – the 'black torture' – from his completed work.

This struggle is written into *Rewards of Wonder* in a variety of ways. Gurney holds up the 'strong Greek things' of Homer and Aeschylus as examples of the kind of aesthetic control to which he aspires; he likewise acclaims Ben Jonson as 'our greatest builder' and Beethoven for having 'our great Ben's mastery'. But he also recognises similar patterns of squareness in the buildings and landscape of the Cotswolds and so celebrates them as an embodiment of the order and harmony that he wishes to impose upon his poetry. This is done directly – Tewkesbury is 'that square thing', whilst the river Severn knows and loves 'strong things' – but also via a series of allusions which acknowledge the historical processes responsible for that order. The majority of these allusions focus on Gloucestershire's Roman inheritance and Gurney's close identification of Rome with ideas of discipline, integrity and regularity; the landscape is for him an ever-present symbol of 'Rome's dignity controlled', making the 'strict Roman honour' it displays a virtue to be both admired and imitated. Indeed, so close is this identification that Gurney frequently uses the word 'Rome' metonymically, so that the presence of such values in things not usually associated with the classical world – 'Beethoven the Roman', for example, or 'Noblest poplars Rome's' – can be immediately appreciated.

But there are also two poems in *Rewards of Wonder* which deal more explicitly with Gurney's battle to turn his schizophrenia to more positive ends. 'What I Will Pay' stresses the strict self-discipline needed to challenge his illness and 'keep thoughts all steady'; only by following a punishing regime which combines physical deprivation with the intensive study of 'masters' such as Bach, Beethoven and Carlyle will he be able to 'write fair on strict thought-pages'. That he feels that he has done so in *Rewards of Wonder* is indicated by 'Poem For End', which closes the collection by celebrating it as a text 'of such grace'. Making explicit what he has previously been content to leave implicit, he draws the reader's attention to 'the wrought out links / Of fancy to fancy' which give the volume its structural and thematic coherence. These complex webs of self-referential allusion are rooted, of course, in the cognitive processes produced by his illness, but he is at pains to stress how he has manipulated them for his own aesthetic purposes, using them to create 'a book' which draws together such seemingly diverse elements as Gloucestershire, France, 'Elizabethans and night-working thoughts' into a consistent, unified narrative.

At the centre of this narrative is Gurney himself – Gurney the artist, Gurney the soldier, Gurney the night-walker – and, more importantly, his conviction that he should be properly rewarded for the sacrifices he has made for his country. Being Gurney, this is not a simple matter of material recompense for his wartime military service; rather, it is part of that elaborate network of beliefs clustered around ideas of beauty, creativity, suffering and recognition which permeate so much of his later work. The most important of these beliefs is Gurney's sense of his own vocation as 'war poet' and self-elected laureate of England. He has prepared himself for these roles by paying 'the prices of life' both in war and peace and he now wants his talent and his calling – his 'right of honour' – to be properly recognised. *Rewards of Wonder*, he believes, will finally prove to 'the sleepers, the custom-followers' that this recognition is long overdue: it is both a celebration of those moments of epiphany granted only to the chosen and the ultimate expression of his abilities as a 'maker'.

But he is also aware, as he says in 'Today', that 'men deny honour as of the spirit of their blood'; worse still, England may have already betrayed his devotion. 'After-War so surely hurt', he writes in 'First Time In' and the sources of this hurt are not hard to find: the unceremonious return home described in 'Blighty', the transformation of Waltheof's field into a rubbish tip in 'The Bargain', his army comrades 'on State-doles, or showing shop-patterns / Or walking town to town sore in borrowed tatterns' in 'Strange Hells'. But what he must have regarded as the greatest betrayal of all is never mentioned. It is only in his appeals for release that he rails against his confinement and expresses his bewilderment that the 'First war poet of England, Maker, nightwalker' (Gurney 10.38) should be treated in this way. Believing as he did that his poetry would help to free him – 'Who, Most kind Lady, has read my poems? Will they not save' he asks Marion Scott in an undated Dartford letter (Gurney 52.11.132) – he knew that such resentment and anger would only detract from what he had managed to achieve in *Rewards of Wonder*. Now, seventy-five years on, it is finally possible to appreciate that achievement in its entirety.

GEORGE WALTER
Lewes 1999

A Note on the Text

This critical edition of *Rewards of Wonder* presents a complete text of the collection itself, together with textual notes indicating the most substantial of Gurney's revisions and various explanatory materials designed to help explain the complex web of biographical, historical and literary allusions which permeate the poems presented here.

The text has been reconstructed from four different sources: the manuscripts produced by Marion Scott for the abortive 1928 Gollancz selection, the Vaughan Williams typescripts, the texts printed by Edmund Blunden in his 1954 selection of Gurney's poems, and the texts published by J C. Squire in the *London Mercury* in January 1924. This has been necessary because Gurney's autograph typescript no longer exists and the Vaughan Williams material – the most substantial surviving copy of *Rewards of Wonder* – is sadly incomplete. Of these four sources, Miss Scott's manuscripts are the most authoritative and have accordingly been used as copy-text wherever possible. Because she only made copies of fifteen out a possible hundred and two texts, however, either the Vaughan Williams typescripts or Blunden's published versions have had to serve as copy-text for the majority of the poems presented here. Squire's texts have only been used when no other appropriate version is available.

The substantives of these texts have not been touched, except where those substantives seem to have been affected by either mistranscription or deliberate interference; in these cases, an alternative reading has been supplied from some other authoritative – usually manuscript – source. Certain accidentals have also been treated in a similar fashion: any capitalisation which does not have an obvious aesthetic function has been removed, whilst the importation by copyists of spellings and forms not usually favoured by Gurney have been emended so that they agree with his usual practice. In 'Old Tale', for example, both Marion Scott and the Vaughan Williams typist change Gurney's 'tire' to 'tyre', but his spelling has been restored here; similarly, the Vaughan Williams typist's emendation of Gurney's 'gray' to 'grey' throughout *Rewards of Wonder* has been corrected. French place-names pose a particular problem in this respect: Gurney's manuscripts show that he wrote 'Buire-au-Bois' both with and without the hyphens and frequently spelt 'La Gorgue' as 'La Gorgues'; rather than choose one form over the other, both forms for each place name have been used here, reflecting Gurney's inconsistent practices. Other accidentals have been emended on purely aesthetic grounds: the titles of poems have been standardised and where Gurney has failed to include closing quotation marks – a frequent practice – these have been added.

One form of accidental, however, has been left largely untouched. The frequency with which Gurney altered his punctuation during his revisions shows that it was an element of his work that was highly important to him Unfortunately, there is now no way of knowing how accurately Gurney's copyists reproduced this aspect of his texts. Faced with this situation, an editor can either reproduce the punctuation in his or her copy-text on the grounds that it is the closest surviving record of what the author may have written, or try to recreate speculatively what that punctuation may have originally looked like. Of course, doing this here runs the risk of actually moving even further away from Gurney's final intentions; accordingly, these texts reproduce his punctuation as it appears in his copyists' renderings of his poems. There is one minor exception to this rule: typists' en dashes have been replaced with em dashes, so as to represent Gurney's ubiquitous use of this punctuation mark more accurately.

Acknowledgements

Many people have helped, either directly or indirectly, in the preparation of this edition. I would like to thank in particular Professor R.K.R. Thornton of the University of Birmingham for both supervising the PhD thesis upon which this book is based and also for his continuing support and encouragement over the years. My thanks are also due to Penny Ely, the Executor of the Gurney Estate, the staff of Gloucester Library for helping me to negotiate the practical aspects of working with Gurney's manuscripts and Henry Buglass for his splendid and enlightening maps.

I am grateful to my fellow Gurney enthusiasts, amongst them Michael Hurd, P.J. Kavanagh and his wife Kate, Pamela Blevins, Anthony Boden, John Phillips and Roderic Dunnett, for their help with this project; my gratitude is also due to all those friends and colleagues who helped to elucidate Gurney's more obscure allusions, in particular Pamela Hinett, Janet Harvey, Alun Howkins, John Jacobs, Rodney Hillman and Stephen Medcalf.

My personal thanks go to Sandra and Dennis O'Leary, Christine Munday, Catherine Small, Ben Scott and, in particular, Anne Johnson for all their help and support. Finally, I would like to dedicate this book to the memory of my father, Jeremy Walter; it would never have appeared were it not for the love and support he gave me when he was alive.

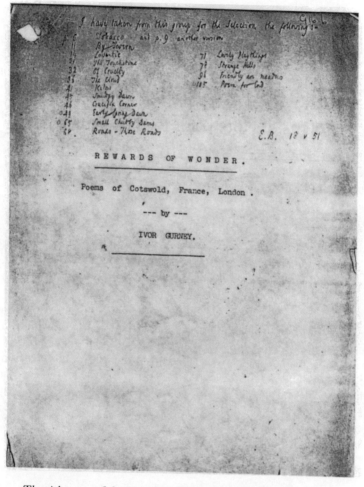

The title page of the Vaughan Williams typescript of Rewards of Wonder, *produced by 'a very good typist in Dorking' in 1943*

REWARDS OF WONDER
Poems of Cotswold, France, London

The Lantern-Shine

The lantern made a green broad radiance
Beneath the pines, a last hour business
Before the farm hand sat in his day's one trance,
Browsing in firelight; and happy in slack-limbedness.

My thoughts had numbed with darkness, my mind had set
And here under pines brightness lit interest in
The blackness; body grew lighter, and owed no debt
Of energy to the brain that all weighed down had been.

The spark of interest hurried onwards expectant thought,
Uphill to Roman things and a road of shadow,
(Where fear was, once men resolutely or carelessly fought) —
Past October's garden of love, past Autumn-crocus meadow,
To the camp white scarred, high in the all-healing night.

October

The sick mind grows whole in October gales
And memory comes
With tides of wind and music whenever fails
The body despises mean men and spirits safe in homes —
Leaves flung riotously and for once carelessly
Send the arm out to touch them lovingly, waveringly;
The blood warms at them — so England's Autumn comes;
And the loves to watch the tossing passion-wind-beaten glooms,
A man's life blessing the tree's life high
A man's music coming out of the war of wind, earth and sky
On Roman and all-powerful rampart outflung —
Fitting the praise of great triumphing night strengths sung

Of Autumn's boyish mood.
When Severn has her Equinoctial flood,
Diurnal turbid glittering in from by Flat Holm
To where the white tower guards a smaller brood
Of churches old when the Free States were young —
Then also — the Cotswold glory fulfils in a story
Of a boy walking tumultuous roads in night-battle of wood
Tossing — Sagas and death songs of Dane, Roman in magnificence
    sung
In the gale finding great glory — and God, Father and Maker good.

Glory — and Quiet Glory

Man takes the heaven of glories for his own,
He limns them out and sings them on stringed wood,
There is no show some master has not made good —
Strength, gratitude, patience has fastened down
To be the wonder and remind to men,
How much blind glory passes by sleepy heads —
And the owl crying menace in the woods
Sees more than that learned man in his close den.
But yet the half things escape and are hardly pondered;
When strict and splendid dawns or lets in roof
Go unheeded — rifts starred on sudden sky like proof —
Armour scoured strictly till the man's eye wondered.
Stubble, light mists, sandweed-rabble, and cathartic flax
Old man's beard that New Year's wind has in tax,
Scabious and trefoil, Edward Thomas beloved poet of all love;
And the forty-eight Preludes and Fugues, and French verse
    unmastered.

Half Dead

Half dead with sheer tiredness, wakened quick at night
With dysentery pangs, going blind among dim sleepers
And dazed into half-dark, illness had its spite.
Head cleared, eyes saw; pangs and ill body-creepers
Stilled with the cold — the cold bringing me sane —
See there was Witcombe Steep as it were, but no beeches there.
Yet still clear flames of stars over the crest bare,
Mysterious glowing on the cloths of heaven,
Sirius or Mars or Argo's stars, and high the Sisters — the Pleiads —
    those seven.

Best turn in, fatigue party out at seven . . . . .
What though beauty was — I had been Cranham's walks . . . . .
Dark was the billet after that seeing of rare
Gold stars, stumbling among the still forms to my lair. —
Still were the stars bright — my sick mind hung on them even.

But long after; in solitary day walking, I recalled
Caulaincourt's Mausoleum and the stars March midnight called;
On the east horizon's dim loveliest shape upheld.
To mix with music in my thought and forget sickness —
To drown sorrow deep that on me was then masterless —
Hunger and weak body and tired mind of needed sleep.
For Argo or Sirius in the East skies or for Regulus.

Tobacco

When tobacco came, when Raleigh did first bring
The unfabled herb; the plant of peace, the known king
Of comfort bringers, then indeed new hope
Came to the host of poets — with new scope,
New range of power, since henceforth one still might sit
Midnight-on and still further, while the war of wit
More kindly became and coloured till dawn came in;
Piercing blind shutter chinks with pale daylight thin,
Talk went on other things than the rich night did relate.

Raleigh he knew, but could not the impossible
War of swift steel and hurtled bronze foretell —
Nor the imaginary hurt on the body's vessel;
Nor how tobacco ever would steady disastered
Nerves, courage by gray terror almost mastered.
Gloucester men, half a day or more; they would hide
Five cigarettes and damp matches well inside
Their breasts, the only thing unsodden, while despair, despair
Dripped incessantly without interest from the air;
Or go supperless
The better next day's tobacco taste to bless.
Wonder at fogs, stars, posts till headaches came
Those chief of trouble-comforts still in number the same. —
Watch Verey lights, sandbags, glasses, rifle sights, mud —
Crampt in uncouth postures men crouched or stood —
A Woodbine breakfast inspiriting the blood.

Or in those caves of dugouts, men talking lazily
Smoke in luxuriously, of Woodbines, Goldflakes easily —
For one gift condoning Fate and its unnatural mazily
Selftangled knots. Easing the strainéd back —
Somehow or other slipping unseen from the rack
Into tobacco scent, or tobacco savour or look; —
The divine virtue of some content long-golden book

Multiplying; or in the sunniest quiet resting
Loll into restlessness or sleepy jesting.
Tobacco truly taken, as poetry, as a real thing.
Tobacco tasted exactly: in waves or odd ring
Noted: tobacco blown to the wind, or still watched
Melt into ether's farthest smother unmatched.
Keen sentries hid whiffing surreptitiously —
Sly fatigue parties hidden from scrutiny —
Last breath favours begged desperately.

Over all the breath of the airy vapour is known.
Life's curtain rises on it and Death's trembles down.
Heroism has taken smoke for sufficient crown.
Wires hang bodies for such courage as makes tobacco so known —
Machine guns sweep in heaps those who such honour keep.

When I think of the Ark slapping hopeless eternal waters —
Of Aeneas' sailors cursed with unclean hunger —
Or Irus and his scorn, or the legions Germanicus
Met, and was nearly scotted by whose just anger;
I know, I realise, and am driven to pity —
As by sun-scorched eternal days of Babylon City —
And any unsoothed war restless people's clamour;
As hunger for Empire, any use of War's evil hammer;
Tea and tobacco after decent day, body-clean labour,
Would bring again England of madrigal, pipe, and tabor —
Merry England again of Daniel, after four centuries,
Of dawn rising and late talking and go-as-you-please.
But by Laventie or Ypres, or Arras the thing
Kept heart and soul together, and the mud out of thinking.
There was no end to the goodness, and Raleigh who journeyed
Far over waters to Virginia — and risked life and there did
Things like the heroes' things — but felt want never as we
Carefully guarding the fragments, and finishing the half spents —
Knew joy never so, nor pain; two hours and miles over sea.
How tell the poetic end and comfort of pain past any sustain?

Laventie Dawn

Dawn came not surprising, but later widened
To great space and a sea of many colours
With slate and pink and blue above the frightened
Mud fields soiled and heavy with War's dolours
And the guns thumped and threatened;
While the bacon frizzled, and the warm incense heightened:
Drifting in bays and dugouts slowly lightened.
Rifles cleaned — and the thought of tea cheered us boys
Who had Cotswold courage — but right love for Cotswold joys
Night lifted off Her gray memory of long dull watching;
And tea, tobacco, delights beyond night's hope matching
Filling minds hungry-empty after the night bare,
And to dodge breakfast with tea and get letters at last,
And to scrawl or read an hour, in content's happy power,
Before the day's useless, absurd danger and hardship,
That began, tea, tobacco, letters — and hope showing clear.

Leckhampton Elbow

Wraith of gray cloud in Leckhampton elbow;
A queer unlooked for relic of short storm
Impelled by air of December — by the stone wonder
Set up high above Shurdington, the meadows so low.
In my mind music gathered of beauty and form:
To see Cotswold cliff standing nobly to wonder
A curious walker, and ready to love — drawing music
And the hidden plain for thought and far Tewkesbury under
Not long the cloud lasted, the mist not thick,
And one might think of old, sacred celebrations
By the strange stone — the worship of mists, or of sun's

Draping or blessing the cliffs, the flat valley with dark or light
Romans who bore noble metals there, ready for fight,
Raising great earth to eternal shapes for lonely shepherds
To wander on, and love in their blood, but find no words . . . .
There are beech woods there, few birds, and the white lazy herds
But Rome, no more than I, unsatisfied with music unwilling,
Had been pleased for Cotswold power less, and her one voice of
   birds.

Tobacco

When tobacco came, when Raleigh first did bring
The herb unfabled, the plant of peace, the king
Of comfort bringers, then indeed new hope
Came to the host of poets with new scope
New range of power, since one henceforth might sit
Till midnight and still further, and the war of wit
More kindly and warm coloured till dawn came in
And pierced the crevices with daylight thin.
Raleigh he knew, but could not the impossible
Terror of flying steel and bronze foretell
Hurtle, scream and impact of today's missile,
Nor the imaginary hurt on the body's vessel.
Raleigh he knew by friendly camp fire, nights round; and took
Company, warmth, wine — gave counsel — with careless joke,
But could not guess that Gloucester men would hide
Five cigarettes a day or more inside
Their breast the one thing unsodden, or go supperless
The better next day's tobacco taste to bless —
Wonder at fogs, stars, posts, till headaches came
To keep those five small tubes in number the same
The Verey lights, grasses, sandbags, rifle-touches, mud —

Crampt in uncouth postures men crouched or stood —
For Woodbine breakfast or the spilling of blood.
Raleigh, rapier or pistolet who handled,
Could not conceive the great cylinder bundled
Incredibly through air, nor the holding off
From imagination the bellow, the blast-cough
Minnie-werfer she had in her cross times,
And what comfort the beloved brown vegetable
Should bring to fear — brave men past soul unable,
Or well had blessed his curling, unmatched fumes
Himself the patron saint of tobacco takers,
Whether on field of battle or in warm-lit rooms.

Queen of Cotswold

Only at certain times the tourists go there,
And the town lives feebly on unemployment pay,
Housed in the old gettings of wool ware,
Wearing such vesture of our Elizabethan day —
And looking for the good times to recover
Some fortune worthy of such nobleness' array.
Splendours gone hollow,
With despair to follow
Heavy on hope not blind to a past of great kind.
Heavy on hearts that loved churches set apart — Beloved
By many a squire and squire's son who had his way
Of tending land, or serving so loved an England — moved
Whether by Northleach, Daylesford or by Massachusetts, Virginia to
    a word.
They took their faith in hand and received just pay.
Names on old honoured tombstones naming known cities.
Families serving the good soil, taming the clay,

These went out — taught by stone
And the Cotswold good done —
Made New States fortunate, Cotswold sad in Her fate.
But now for love and good of Cotswold
Now to untold
Barrenness and uselessness fallen, where a reverent walker
May bring a clean small money to some waiting woman;
Or give a man a week's hope of work fit for human,
And with a pleased town-dweller be pleasant talker.

By Severn

If England, her spirit lives anywhere
It is by Severn, by hawthorns and grand willows.
Earth heaves up twice a hundred feet in air
And ruddy clay falls scooped out to the weedy shallows.
There in the brakes of May Spring has her chambers,
Robing-rooms of hawthorn, cowslip, cuckoo flower —
Wonder complete changes for each square joy's hour,
Past thought miracles are there and beyond numbers.
If for the drab atmospheres and managed lighting
In London town, Oriana's playwrights had
Wainlode her theatre and then coppice clad
Hill for her ground of sauntering and idle waiting.
Why, then I think, our chiefest glory of pride
(The Elizabethans of Thames, South and Northern side)
Would nothing of its meeding be denied,
And her sons' praises from England's mouth again be outcried.

The Tax Office

Georgian with a stairway up to the roof
And banisters of carved and curious grace . . .
An Inspector saw it, liked light and open space.
Bespoke it. 'Office of Taxes' is the proof.
And puzzled country folk climb stair with forms,
Inquire of rebates, and fend imagined harms,
In the rooms some man planned as his poetry's mind so
Fancied — 'In this way, and in this way my house should go.'
And here the Gloucester farmers bring State-dues in
What strength and cunning could from bare earth outwin.
Winter light shines rosy on the oaken stairway
As Summer floods with true gold universal day
Throwing slant light on forms and piles of stiff forms,
On polished surfaces and mixed-up heaped-like-hay
Envelope piles, drear walls and the mixed harms
Of three times fifty years.
Sunshine falls there
The imagined graces of West Country air
Are a loved thing there —
On clerks at worrying method into service order:
And on the border
Of the precincts of secrecy the line
Everchanging of iniquity-fearing
Liable citizens wearing
Faces of anxiousest mien
Turning to go out then, at last to return to
Real lands whose name in writing is sudden freedom
For clerks writing dumb;
Looking out suddenly on river or new
Cornland, or dry stubble as the new season leads
Figures of acres, records of deeds of meads
By Waltheof or Egbert held perpetually
(Since service paid) for some unfelt nominal fee.
Seeing beyond paper marked clerkly the history

Of rich flats of Severn or Uptons in writ-free
Poplar'd closes, May with dim November (and feast-time December)
Loves: they are at home there. They are loved equally.
Autumn hears talk there of June's breath-tossed wild hedge-roses;
And Autumn crocus dies not at March's violet loveliness.
The earth has such memory — nothing dies, nothing in thought does
    die.

Praise of Tobacco

Great Jonson praised tobacco as was fit,
So great a thing come new in so late time.
(What! Israel and Rome and Charlemagne not ever to have heard the
    name?)
But I with imitative and halting wit,
Would still set words in rows and edged with rhyme
To say an admiration after his great precedition.
But with more right, who by Laventie have smoked, and made —
Smoked and by Arras remembered the writer's trade.
Longer than he (but not so worthy that ended
His Spaniard foe, as noble as honour demanded).
But with more right, for I have read Scott and smoked —
And Hardy — and sailed to Bollo, felt keel there jerked . . .
Belloc and Bach and Brahms, and the dear Beethoven.
Read poets of France, of earth love and sound love woven —
And after Carlyle, his honour and hard courage worked.
And smoked by Vermand and Temple Street steps and high Beacons
Of Cotswold, under such stars as none ever saw moving
So high and clear: Winter, Summer, Cotswold, and at all hours of all
    seasons,
And gone where the spirits of Roman sentinels loved me and lurked.

Laventie

One would remember still
Meadows and low hill
Laventie was, as to the Line and elm row
Growing through green strength wounded, as home elms grow.
Shimmer of Summer there and blue Autumn mists
Seen from trench-ditch winding in mazy twists.
The Australian gunners in close flowery hiding
Cunning found out at last, and smashed in the unspeakable lists.
And the guns in the smashed wood thumping and griding.

The letters written there, and received there,
Books, cakes, cigarettes in a parish of famine,
And leaks in rainy times with general all-damning.
The crater, and carrying of gas cylinders on two sticks
(Pain past comparison and far past right agony gone,)
Strained hopelessly of heart and frame at first fix.

Café-au-lait in dugouts on Tommies' cookers,
Cursed minnie-werfs, thirst in eighteen hour summer.
The Australian miners clayed, and the being afraid
Before strafes, sultry August dusk time than Death dumber —
And the cooler hush after the strafe, and the long night wait —
The relief of first dawn, the crawling out to look at it,
Wonder divine of Dawn, man hesitating before Heaven's gate.
(Though not on Cooper's where music fire took at it,
Though not as at Framilode beauty where body did not shake at it.)
Yet the dawn with aeroplanes crawling high at Heaven gate
Lovely aerial beetles of wonderful scintillate
Strangest interest, and puffs of soft purest white —
Soaking light, dispersing colouring for fancy's delight.

Of Maconachie, Paxton, Tickler, and Gloucester's Stephens;
Fray Bentos, Spiller and Baker, odds and evens
Of trench food, but the everlasting clean craving

For bread, the pure thing, blessèd beyond saving.
Canteen disappointments, and the keen boy braving
Bullets or such for grouse roused surprisingly through
(Halfway) Stand-to.
And the shell nearly blunted my razor at shaving;
Tilleloy, Fauquissart, Neuve Chapelle, and mud like glue.

But Laventie, most of all, I think is to soldiers
The Town itself with plane trees, and small-spa air;
And vin, rouge-blanc, chocolats, citron, grenadine:
One might buy in small delectable cafés there.
The broken church, and vegetable fields bare;
Neat French market town look so clean,
And the clarity, amiability of North French air.
Like water flowing beneath the dark plough and high Heaven,
Music's delight to please the poet pack-marching there.

April is Happy

April is happy now her sowing's done
And the cloak hangs ready in her own room.
May may take over all she does possess
But with courtesy also and shamefastness.

The brake, the coppice, the meadow, the lane
As last year, are made new lovely again,
And the boy May ambitious finds nothing to do,
In a week's time crowned, and a night-walker prince to view.

The Ford

As any blue thing can be the ford was good,
The time was March, after snow, amiable of mood,
Between storm and tomorrow's storm, and the Company
Hauling and lifting saw between their struggles the
Road and very passage Agincourt's Companies
Avoided Fate by, and had their own hard degrees
Of trouble, and hauling, shifting of baggages.

But were they hungry, hungry and weak as we were?
And had the same cursings, longings to be well clear
Of the whole business, to be away, to be back again,
Tired of the whole paraphernalia of varied pain?
Tired of being tired, and being without beds,
Of fear and misery — tangle and loggerheads?

And saw the blue ford, did they, and remembered sudden
A Winter flooding on the little Leadon
Or Windrush? where the meadows squelch and quake beneath;
Or Brimscombe with its pines and midnight wood edge beech
    wooden.
Forgot the chance of losing them so, of very death, very death.
Drawing the heart and eyes together with unfelt breath.

The Bargain

It was agreed that Carthage should be rased
When Rome her strength to nervelessness has braised.
But what compact had Britain with the West or South
When Spain's pride whelmed all in the Atlantic's mouth?
The pageantry and panoply and pennonry

All sea-wrack, hung on broad reef and granite tooth.
So square a fate no Spanish sage clear divined.
No rumour of Resolutest Fates combined
To shatter oak and iron on Hebrides and Galway —
For months to move unending on the green tides alway,
Till the fisher-folk or the peasants rescued wood for the blind
Night, and made bright fire of what England might have made
    conquer.
No compact with the wind or rough seas, God wrought
And Drake and Hawkins sailed artist wise and fought,
And there was matchless skill from Devon to Thames mouth,
Light guns and heavy guns belching smoke and death out,
The wonder of great sails showing above the Atlantic tides,
And Bristol men against Cadiz giving shout for shout
While the land trembled, and new Churches to their known Builder
    prayed.

Darkness Has Cheating Swiftness

Darkness has cheating swiftness
When the eyes rove,
Opens and shuts in long avenues
That thought cannot prove.

Darkness shuts in and closes;
There are three ghosts
Different in one clump of hedge roses,
And a threat in posts —

Till one tops the road crest,
Turns, sees the city lie
Long stretched out in bright sparkles of City decency,
Homecalling, far away.

Student Days

When a cloud is not on the mind the sky clouds
The alternate fortunes darken as Cotswold shrouds
In January; Cooper's and Painswick never are seen
At one time blown, as most fitting, all weather clean.

So it seemed one time at Gloucester, in my music time,
In joy's mood — rain came, it beat on my showing hair
Spite kindly — but my hair and my spirit were dear
To me then: the feel of both in my being — on the turf and lime.

But I was young, and working as I best could
With dear friends, and a piano would say the furthest
Thing that my spirit thought — and could mock at roughest
Wind of Cotswold — friend of wrath in the rocking wood.

The Ford

A million men before me had taken those steps
And thought those thoughts, looked over to the brick ferry,
But none so cracked as I in cross fate perhaps,
And yet a drink rights all, good coffee or good perry.

Danes had passed there, Roman heights east and west.
They too had tugged at oars — or stood watchful in exile
Guarding a land dear to them — and seen need clear to them guest.
Good coffee or good perry is more than a fool's light whim.

The Touchstone (Watching Malvern)

What Malvern is the day is, and its touchstone —
Gray velvet, or moon-marked; rich, or bare as bone;
One looks towards Malvern and is made one with the whole;
The world swings round him as the Bear to the Pole.

Men have crossed seas to know how Paul's tops Fleet,
That as music has rapt them in the mere street,
While none or few will care how the curved giants stand,
(Those upheaved strengths!) on the meadow and plough-land.

Thoughts of New England

Gloucester streets walking in Autumn twilight,
Past Kineburgh's cottage and old Raven Tavern,
That Hoare he kept, the Puritan, who tired
Or fired, and took a passage in the 'Mayflower',
Gloucester streets walking in frost-clear hour —
Of *Captains Courageous* as a boy read, thinking,
And sea-ports, ships, and all that boy desired . . .
Walt Whitman, history-scraps and Huck Finn's cavern:
My thoughts went wondering how the New England Folk
Walked twilight now, watched stars steady or blinking —
If thoughts came Eastward as mine Westward went.
Of our *Citizen*, the *Massachusetts Times*,
And the boys crying them perhaps about their lanes.
But those no historied ground of Roman or Danes.

What are the streets that have no memories,
That are not underset by ancient rubbish?
Where gables overhang, and the quarters clang

From Cathedral towers, and the slops or dinner dish,
Hurried a man voids handily in the gutter:
And ghosts haunt the streets and of old troubles mutter.
Where steel and scarlet of the military
And routine use flash vivid momentarily;
Imagination stricken unaccountably
At full day into pictures not looked for even,
And children from their play by curfew driven.

Are there men of my blood over Atlantic
Wondering there what light is growing thick
By Severn and what real thing Cotswold is?
Are there men walking slow till tiredness leads in
To write or read till the night's veil grows thin;
Insatiate desiring what hope would win?
Is the air clear there as Thoreau's prose,
With frost and sparkling water, and day's close
As mild, as soft as shows in *Evangeline*?
(Since all verse from the air or earth does win.)

Do they hear tell of Domesday Book, and not
Think of this Gloucester where the scrivener wrote
Command of reeves first set their lists to begin?
Do they wish walk at evening where the earls went in
And William: Are there not crowns of England old
That first in Gloucester's Abbey showed their gold?
Can villas contain man in unloving hold
As here the cornered, the nooked low-ceilinged beetle-browed
Houses cloak man in; or the strict thoroughfares
Stone or asphalt-paved ally to man?

Are there great joys in April her high days
For those who cannot high imaginations see
Of other men builded, stirred to a great praise?
Cotswold earthing profound for white material,
Masses of stone gone slender as a silver birch,
Upwards in dazzle to an arching azure.

O where in the New World shall recompense come,
For the market-days, the week-end trouble without measure,
The crowded four ways and cattle markets boom,
And country faces seen often with so much pleasure?

Can New England think deep thoughts of her bye-ways,
Is Abanar and Pharpar a balance for
Severn receiving Avon, at her knot of highways,
Her Abbey township, beneath so high a cloud floor?

But nevertheless one would go very willingly
At the year's turn, where Washington or Lincoln walked,
Or praise *Drum Taps* or 'This Compost', and hear talked
Speech of Lowell, or Hawthorne, or Holmes and be
Pleased with citizenship of Gloucester or Worcester
And companionship of veterans or veterans' sons
Of the Wilderness or Richmond, see the old guns
That set Chattanooga's thronged woods astir;
Or woke terror in steadfastness with red anger.

But not for longer than the strangeness lasted.
Severn yet calls not to be resisted:
And the mix of Dane thoughts, Roman, with Middle-Age
Calls all love out to mark on any page
The glory of Peter's Abbey high in Summer,
Or low in Winter's gloom, and a wavering shape,
Are more than is ever seen by foreign comer
To Connecticut, or Staten or Providence with its cape,
Being loveliness and history and height in one.

And there is nothing uprooted that is not changed.
Better to stay and wonder in the half light
How New England saunters where Kipling loved and ranged,
And watch the starling flocks in first Autumn flight.

The New World has qualities its own,
But the Old not yet decrepit or withered is grown,
And brick and timber of age five centuries known
Are consolation for poverty enough
Against New York, where they say Opera is brilliant,
And the byeways with five dollar notes are strown.
The stuff of Liberty is a varying stuff,
But from Grant's men, Lee's men, nobleness should never want.

When The Sun Leaps Tremendous

When the sun leaps tremendous from the rim
Of sea or land the birds have awoken yet hours.
All but the townsfolk look out to welcome him
And the Great Sun is glad for such eyes of welcome.
Friendly to children, and who keeps child hearts of home.
But City people keep shameful soft beds in brick
And slate erections polite, set far too thick.
Sleep because others sleep, and have regular meals —
Not imagining how Orion or Arcturus or the Great Bear wheels.
Or what under their influence comes beauty unworded from
    nowhence,
Withy and goldcups — and trefoil, Rome's dignity controlled.
The quiet determination of the earth for beauty of Her own.
Wonderful as the sun.
Earth's quiet challenge to the great Fire of Heaven aloft and all-bold;
Trefoil, the unheeded, friend of Caesar for courage and virtue
    untold.

Canadians

We marched, and saw a Company of Canadians
Their coats weighed eighty pounds at least, we saw them
Faces infinitely grimed in, with almost dead hands
Bent, slouching downwards to billets comfortless and dim.
Cave dwellers last of tribes they seemed, and a pity
Even from us just relieved (much as they were), left us.
Somme, what a desolation's damned land, what iniquity
Of mere being. There of what youth that country bereft us;
Plagues of evil lay in Death's Valley we also had
Forded that up to the thighs in chill mud almost still-stood
As they had gone — and endured day as night without sun.
Gone for five days then any sign of life glow
As the notched stumps or the gray clouds (then) we stood;
Dead past death from first hour and the needed mood
Of level pain shifting continually to and fro.
Saskatchewan, Ontario, Quebec, Stewart White ran in
My own mind; what in others? These men who finely
Perhaps had chosen danger for reckless and fine chance
Fate had sent for suffering and dwelling obscenely
Vermin eaten, fed beastly, in vile ditches meanly.
(Backwoods or clean Quebec for defiled, ruined, man-killing France)
And the silver thrush no more crying Canada — Canada for the
    memory.

Severn Meadows

Soft veils of dusk wrapping Severn meadows
And anything of mystery in the shadows,
This was of old time, now is the terror gone
Of inquisition into dear Night's tender own.

To catch the lightning in a foolish loop
Is a trick, and Caspian into Sahara to scoop,
Severn meadows are true poet's test at last
And the best fury October there in full clean blast,
How leaves go whirling by Longford Park house high east!

After War — Half War

One got peace of heart at last, the dark march over,
And the straps slipped, the body felt under roof's low cover,
Lying slack the body, being let sink into straw giving;
And some sweetness, a great sweetness felt in mere living.
And to come to this haven after sorefooted weeks,
The dark barn roof, and the glows and the wedges and bright streaks,
Candles and gold light — tea for the body's delight,
Letters from home, dry warmth and still sure rest taken
Sweet to the chilled frame, nerves soothed were so sore shaken.
(It was after Tilleloy's strafing for one whole week, and straw
Is Heaven's rest — after marching numb — and knowing but Army
    law.)

The Ford

As any blue thing can be the ford was blue,
In the March light; afterglow and all washed through
Between storm and next storm while the Company
Hauling and lifting saw between their struggling lie
The irregular azure water below lit clear with bright sky.
Rest for a moment, then more struggling with rough beams
Or bricks to be roadmended in gaping. Lovely March lit
With azure darlingness the shapes and whole of it.
And after so much cold, and sleet raining at the bold
Unshielded face of marching Infantry, weak, moving free
(My Infantry, My Gloucesters, heart's hope to me).
Brought out of Cotswold earth, of Stroud Valley clay —
Or by some clean blood father by-Severn way.
The water below there, natural lovely indeed after
The trenches of mud evil past any thought of disaster
Of facing Germans — once mud had rotted the soul.
Until the frost killed care, and we'd have died without fail
Rather than give an inch to any worst enemy.
Because after loathing, frost froze the sense away.
The Blue Ford — Henry crossed near there after I read —
In after times but to late to help; the lovely all azuréd
Water and the brown slope — March kind after so cruel a way.

Laventie Front

One would remember still
The meadows and low hill
Laventie was, as to the Line, and elm row
Growing as sweet in wounds as home trees grow.
(But hurt and fearing as we — shell bursts and shrapnel.)

The Summer shimmer there and Autumn mists
Seen from trenches of red soil and many twists
Past the Australian gunners in close hiding
Cunning at length found, smashed, in the unspeakable lists.
(Courage unmatched against Aubers batteries and all seeing posts.)
Tea, the blessedest thing of all Line comforts,
All-need-meeting brewage of infinite sorts;
All one, and tobacco right ration of endurance,
To sight smell touch satisfaction and sustenance —
The hungriness gone questing to all climes
All countries for consolation in cold times.
(Aubers terrors drove us in mind to Cotswold kind)
The nerve-struck fear on tenth days, the thirst, soreness, tiredness —
Gone out to beauty for consoling tenderness;
And the ache of labour carried beyond hunger.
Despair below, hidden over by events stronger.
And of the dawns gone upwards in dim curtain-wise;
First guess, first sureness, milk light, and recognise
Of aeroplanes, faint bright wonders of high sunrising.
Above stillness penetrated and hit through, or surely threated
With cannon voice of terror and quick surprising.
All in the Atlantic dawns of North France — Her lands.
The common danger of the Line which none will believe
For envy of honour's sake — or for stupidity honour to grieve.
Of letters never known precious so before in history —
Save to the Ark, what boon of grace these be
(The opening of crammed stockings on Christmas dawn
Or high poetry's significance seen first amazed.)
Bacon's smell gone from breakfast, scant bread drawn as
Strange rare substance received, touched, and praised:
Crumb by crumb imagined and to imagination raised.
Noman's, like any gas works of drear environs;
With scrawls of wire, and deadness and upright irons
Aubers Ridge on, elms and the sun face behind them moved
Upward and upward till full July day was proved.
And the Riez Bailleul woods were looked down on and loved.

Cyril Tourneur

Cyril Tourneur, avid of name and fame,
The applause of theatres and note of theatres' crowds
With knife and bowl — shade of Hell's murkiest clouds
Would with rant-dialogue make an immortal name:
Drinking at Southwark: with quick eyes and gibing talk,
Poets, prentices, a young squire, and seamen gay —
Of Samuel Daniel's goldenest lines and walk
With fine ladies, and each having written his play,
On Juliet the talk, or Greene's way; of Celia later
And Jonson's Fulvia, when Tourneur boasted, 'I could
As brave lines make on a street girl as Cleopatra Her chatter,
That Egypt's queen, and in my bread-earning day-by-day mood,'
But knew his heart must pay for so high a heart's matter
And paid — Lamb caught at immortality, finding it good,
And 'cloth of silver' clothes the word 'slut' for ever.

Of Cruelty

From the racked substance of the earth comes the plant and
That with heat and the night frost is tortured:
To some perfection that grows, man's thought wills his hand —
Roots rent, crown broken, grub holed, it is drawn upward.

A hundred things since the first stir have hunted it,
The rooks any time might have swallowed ungrateful,
Caterpillars, slugs, as it grew, have counted on it,
And man the planter bent his gaze down on it fateful.

The thing will go to market, it must be picked up and loaded,
The salesman will doubt it or chuck it anyway in,
A horse must be harnessed first, or a donkey goaded
Before the purchaser may ever the first price pay for it.

Who may be now trembling with vast impatience
And anxieties and mixed hopes for a resurrection
Out of the mouldering soul — to be new form, have perfections
Of flowers and petal and blade, to die, to be born to clean action.

First March

It was first marching, hardly had we settled yet
To think of England, or escaped body pain —
(Cotswold or music — or poetry, the pack to forget)
Flat country going leaves but small chance, small hope for
The mind to escape to any resort but its vain
Own circling grayness and stain;
First halt, second halt, and then to spoiled country again.
There were unknown kilometres to march, one must settle
To play chess, or talk home talk, or think as might happen
After three weeks of February frost few were in fettle,
Barely frost bite the most of us Gloucesters had escapen.
To move, then, to go onward, at least to be moved —
Myself had revived and then dulled down. It was I
Who stared for body-ease on the gray sky
And watched in grind of pain the monotony
Of grit, road metal, slide underneath by, dull down by,
To get there being the one thought under, to get marching done.

Suddenly, a road's turn brought the sweet unexpected
Pleasure. Snowdrops bloomed in a ruined garden neglected:

Roman the road; as of Birdlip we were on the verge,
And this West Country thing so from chaos to emerge
(Surely Witcombe with dim water lay under March's morning-
    falter?)
One gracious touch the whole wilderness corrected.

But words are only words and the snowdrops were such
Then, as some Bach fugue wonder — or some Winter Tale touch.

Of Bricks and Brick Pits

Of the kilns that saw the Siege, that saved England,
Of the bricks that re-made all that in manner grand
Citizens broke down, blew up, in the first round.

Of Westgate Street, glorification of fine clay,
Beyond the later horrors of a meaner day,
And the romantic withy pits becoming all grown
Over with willow, plane, ash and the up-and-down
Hardly ever resting regiments of ranged sedges —
In lines, in squares and any-ordered wedges,
Where moorhens startle, squattering etched lines.

Some brain or other will conceive new material
Manufacture odds and ends of waste into
Square or oblong chunks of family mansion,
Some Town Councillor dignity to make proud and fulfil.
Gray or dull white or evil-looking blue, and new.
Severn kilns will blaze bright at night no longer and
The city rubbish will fill the meadows with convenient
Villas to hide the grass up, and to be ugly and to stare and stand.

Cotswold Slopes

Wonderful falls makes Cotswold edge, it drops
From the roadway, or quarry or young beech copse
It gestures, and is below in a white flash
Of lucky places. But where the roadways clash
By Frocester Hill, flatness is flatness' self,
With thorn bushes and rabbits in haunt of elf
And kind hobgoblin continual corners:
Where rest calls out to beggars and seldom sorners;
Working or walking their way through the June's palaces
To red-brick dosshouses or the cheaper workhouses.
While here all wonder with clean sheets spreads a pallet
Tiredness to soak content, no ill to befall it;
Swept over all night by soft wrapping dim airs . . .
Till dawn takes one onward a mile, and the day-lit
Cotswold shows all that County, with towns and inns:
Tunes and tales in the quick mind eager desire begins;
Who walked here, and debated his sword, or who walked poor
    student to Oxford,
Who debated a country's fate and kept Death in heart unfeared
What squire watched his loved land, and cared for his hid ways and
    cairn stand?
The beech copses are they not better than thorn, confess!
And the flat thousand foot up plain, whose barns
Front light like Thebes' self or strength of Timgad
Runs on to waterless, treeless gray spaces,
And to acre ploughlands square with gray walls — Cotswold walls —
And light mists on the commons and fallow sad places
With some change seen in the grass-colours and farm faces.
And O Cotswold! but your morning . . . your love's light lucent,
Friendly milkness of white when all-day's spread over
Cover and haunt of plover, where the lone drover
Thinks of the walker, and wishes he too were free
Rather than tend sheep or make fruitful Cotswold earth for grain,
Or against night inclement lop bough from the fallen tree.

Robecq

Robecq, that's all swept away now, so men tell,
Is but the lightest hint of what was well.
Memory to fact — Robecq the name — such taste
Of sound stays hidden subtle and grows-there fast —
As a thought of skies, a girl's way and inn's shelter.
Poplars coloured, and holy in memory of All Hallows
A bell and white Merville dreaming still over the fallows.

Near Vermand

Lying flat on my belly shivering in clutch-frost,
There was time to watch the stars, we had dug in:
Looking eastward over the low ridge; March scurried its blast
At our senses, no use either dying or struggling.
Low woods to left — (Cotswold Her spinnies if ever)
Showed through snow flurries and the clearer star weather,
And nothing but chill and wonder lived in mind; nothing
But loathing and fine beauty, and wet loathéd clothing.
Here were thoughts. Cold smothering and fire-desiring,
A day to follow like this or in digging or wiring.
Worry in snow flurry and lying flat, flesh the earth loathing.
I was forward sentry and would be relieved
In a quarter or so, but nothing more better to crouch
Low in the scraped holes and to have frozen and rocky couch —
To be by desperate home thoughts clutched at, and heart-grieved.
Was I ever there — a lit warm room and Bach, to search out sacred
Meaning; and to find no luck; and to take love as believed.

The Cloud

One could not see or think, the heat overcame one,
With a dazzle of square road to challenge and blind one,
No water was there, cow parsley the only flower
Of all May's garland this torrid before-Summer hour,
And but one ploughman to break ten miles of solitariness.
No water, water to drink, stare at, the lovely clean grained one.

Where like a falcon on prey, shadow flung downward
Solid as gun-metal, the eyes sprang sunward
To salute the silver radiance of an Atlantic high
Prince of vapour required of the retinue
Continual changing of the outer-sea's flooding sun
Cloud royal, born called and ordered to domination,
Spring called him out of his tent in the azure of pleasure,
He girt his nobleness — and in slow pace went onward
A true monarch of air chosen to service and station;
And directed on duties of patrolling the considered blue.
But what his course required being fulfilled, what fancy
Of beyond-imagination did his power escape to
With raiment of blown silver . . . .

At the Inn

Alas, for the singers, who might vamp chords
Underneath the broad tune and the jolly words.
Twenty men willing, but skill is hardly
Linked up with kindness, fingers move frowardly,
Frosty the air, and my fingers not ready for keys,
But 'Widdicome Fair' was easy — and would always please,
'I'm Seventeen Come Sunday', 'Furze' and grand 'Spanish Sailors'
On Cotswold these should have welcome always and manly hearers.

Cold left my blood, I was in desired company,
With Bardolph's friends and Drayton's, fire comforted me,
Blaze lit warmth; warmth moved my love's mind to more love:
To midnight so might the talking hours, with stars above, move.

Of Trees Over There

There were Ypres trees as bad as cabbage stumps
Spoiled great things, but unsightly lumps and humps:
And of plane trees, route march and of stroll the borders:
For the straight traffic-roads (Napoleon's orders)
Between Arras and Ypres green border ribbons
(Lovely plane trees shaking their green leaves against blue heavens
    seen).
Footweary soldiers travelled on, transport and guns,
Riders and marchers taking strength from those trees.
Canal of loved Merville, La Gorgues much like to these.
Silver birch of Aveluy's valley remembered northward
In the swamps of azure and scattered emerald keeping guard,
Noblest poplars Rome's leaving by Riez Bailleul
And Buire-au-Bois great elms of pride ancestral
That the sun loved; the winter trees near Creçy village,
Where the crescent hung and dreamed in twiggy cradle,
(Slung above January earth above the brown tillage),
Sliding from rest to rest without fear to fall.
But I remember as well as any the changing Autumn
Poplars of Robecq village at All Souls' time,
As soft and bold as bronze gongs softly smitten or men's far songs
Roman, Christian, Sun worshippers; and I in rhyme
Tried to make show the spreading beauty of them:
By Death his hand touched tenderly to unwritten, unforgotten
Calm happiness of colour,
Robecq, Merville, Riez Bailleul in the North France Autumn.

Gifts and Courtesy

Mostly I remember high days and afterglows
Sound sleep, gray tiredness, and sudden calls
To fatigues or night work, and the unspeaken throes
Of one gas cylinder fatigue, and comradeship, and danger
When Aubers or Passchendaele burst out terribly in anger.

But I remember one time a kindness done
By a signaller who took six hours more duty on
That I should sleep or read — as I had best heed
The Company poet, not looking ever to get print, be read.

And French soldiers kindly, veterans of Hugo's pages,
Women tending us, with faces as out of Gaul's ages,
And Flemish peasant careless of danger by Ypres rages.

The Welsh regiment who took us in — the signallers
Sang soft Welsh songs lovely to my hungry heart and ears,
And there was a hostess of La Gorgues, another of Buire-au-Bois,
Coffee one gave — a poem: the other lovely salad of so
Grateful touch — after bully and biscuits for weeks,
Kindness enough for twenty — woman's tending heart that speaks.

And stars of October Tilleloy, and March Artois,
September Robecq — that stay longer than grief or woe —
And Ypres ghastly made Romance in September's red glow,
Bringing home longing hot to the soldiers thronging
Thick for Death between Somme Farm and the cemetery's faint
    show.

Roman, and the War Poet

There is a scorn of mankind in the short grassed
Cotswold slopes that scabious flower loving to man
Would try to hide; the past, only the still past
Will that green-grayness accept in its stretching plan.

'Armour, and discipline and all night watching
Such men of arms and poetry get welcome here.
Go you down, shelter from weather under stone slab or thatching,'
There is scorn there even for walkers not given to fear.

But I had read Plutarch, and most glorious Antony,
Beethoven the Roman, and Jonson were friends to me —
Having no more fear than Cato of Rome the dear —
Her pretended strictness — denied by me, as comradely —
Brutus or Maximus and Cato my friends by camps there.

And as for arms, I had known more of hard danger
Than any of those drilled legionaries that here were ranger
And was war poet — my wounded arm flung challenge to their
    trodden earth there.

Kilns

Severn has kilns set all along her banks
Where the thin reeds grow and rushes in ranks;
And the carts tip rubbish there from the town;
It thunders and raises white smoke and goes down.
I think some of those kilns are very old,
An age is on those small meres, and could unfold
Tales of many tenders of kilns and tales,

Of the diggers and earth delvers of those square weals
Or oblong of Severn bank. And all the flowers
June ever imagined stand and fulfil June's hours.
I think of the countless slabs gone out from all of them;
Farm house, cottage, loved of generations of men,
Fronting day as equal, or in dusk shining dim;
Of the Dane-folk curious of the sticky worthy stuff;
Kneading, and crumbling till the whim wearied enough.
Of the queer bricks unlearned hands must have made;
Spoiling clay, wasting wood, working out the war's trade;
With one hand the clear eyes fending, keeping in shade
Fierce Fire that grazes and melts with its regardings rough.
Or the plays children had of Dane-Saxon breed,
Chasing round the square kilns with devil-may-care
Headlong roughness of heedless body-reckless speed;
Grazing knees and knuckles to disaster there.
Of the creeping close to parents when November azure
Melancholy made company, and stillness, new pleasure,
And the wonder of fire kept the small boys to stay sure.

And the helping of fathers build well of the new brick,
The delight in handling over thin and thick — the youthful critic.

Of the Normans, how they liked kilns, that thrust to endure
Endless abbeys and strong chapels up in the air,
And Domesday questioners who worried the too evasive
Owner as to tales and days' work to a story unplausive,
As to the fuels used, and the men there and the hours, the wage
    hours.

Riez Bailleul

Riez Bailleul in blue tea-time
Called back the Severn lanes, and roads
Where the small ash leaves lie, and floods
Of hawthorn leaves turned with night's rime,
No Severn though nor great valley clouds.

Now in the thought comparisons
Go with those here-and-theres and fancy
Sees on the china firelight dancy
The wall lit where the sofa runs.
A dear light like Sirius or Spring sun's.

But the trench thoughts will not go, tomorrow
Up to the Line; and no straw laid
Soft for the body, and long night's dread
Lightless, all common human sorrow.
(Unploughed the grown field once was furrow).

Meanwhile soft azure; the Fall's dusk clear
Lovely the road makes, a softness clings
Of colour and texture of light; there rings
Metal, as it were, in air, and the called
Of Twilight, dim stars of the dome appear.

So why muse more in the way of poet?
Lonely — when wine of estaminets
Was red to the spirit as to the gaze,
Golden the lamplight and boys who knew it,
Poets leave stars then, go human ways.

Riez Bailleul Also

There's dusk here; West hedgerows show thin:
In billets there's sound of packs reset,
Tea finished; the dixies dried of the wet,
Some walk, some write, and the cards begin,
Stars gather in heaven and the pools drown in,
And I must walk to ponder of music alone
Another to think of girl or mother, and have done,
To dread Lights-Out like evil (to the strict Gloucesters),
Pain-cleansed thoughts of England, Her young soldiers
Under stars to be lonely for a while, sorrow-vext, then drown deep
    from fears.

What I Will Pay

What I will pay to my God is that I will not sleep between sheets,
Neither take rest unwanted, but work till the first small bird fleets
Past my window, to take rest then (new power); and to take it
    walking,
To be of first flowers a friend — and to noble tree-trunks talking.
Resting so, without ever closing the eyes or at all
Ceasing from work till need or gratitude gives the word, and my soul.
To praise God in sound or words — and to follow masters,
Beethoven, Bach, Jonson — keeping any safe, clear from disasters.
To watch trees and stone, others asleep, and see them alone,
There to learn truth and beauty — and be holier — then be gone.
To keep strict thought — to honour, and have no envy;
To honour water of a morning, and to lave my fair clean body.
Tea and tobacco and my masters, the Elizabethans and Bach my
    food,

Drink when I would — to have Carlyle his thought of good, and by
    wood
Stone, iron, earth, air, water; to keep thoughts all steady to ages,
To start day at dawn's wind, and write fair on strict thought-pages.
These prices to have paid were enough for Shakespeare or Borrow,
Their God, or of Homer — and might Gloucestershire guard from
    all sorrow.

Smudgy Dawn

Smudgy dawn scarfed with military colours
Northward, and flowing wider like slow sea water,
Woke in lilac and elm and almost among garden flowers.
Birds a multitude; increasing as it made lighter.
Nothing but I moved by railings there; slept sweeter
Than Kings the country folk in thatch or slate shade.
Peace had the gray West fleece clouds sure in its power —
Out on much-Severn I thought waves readied for laughter,
And the fire-swinger promised behind the elm-pillars
A day worthy such beginning to come after.
To the room then to work with such hopes as may
Come to the faithful night worker, in West Country's July.

Crucifix Corner

There was a water dump there and regimental
Carts came every day to line up and fill full
Those rolling tanks with chlorinated clay mixture
And curse the mud with vain veritable vexture.
Aveluy across the valley, billets, shacks, ruins.
With time and time a crump there to mark doings.
On New Year's Eve the marsh gloomed tremulous
With rosy mist still holding so marvellous
Sunglow; the air smelt home; the time breathed home —
Noel not put away; New Year's Eve not yet come.
All things said 'Severn', the air was of those dusk meadows —
Transport rattled somewhere in southern shadows
Stars that were not strange ruled the lit tranquil sky,
Arched far and high.

What should break that but gun-noise or last Trump?
Neither broke it. Suddenly at a light jump
Clarinet sang into 'Hundred Pipers and A''
Aveluy's pipers answered with pipers' true call
'Happy we've been a' tegether' when nothing, nothing
Stayed of war-weariness or Winter-loathing.
Cracker with stockings hung in the quaint Heavens
Orion and the seven stars comical at odds and evens —
Gaiety split discipline in sixes or sevens —
Hunger mixed strangely with magical leavens.
It was as if Cinderella had opened the Ball
And music put aside the time's saddened clothing.
It was as if Sir Walter were company again
In the late night — *Antiquary* or *Midlothian* —
Or *Redgauntlet* bringing Solway clear to the mind.
After music, and a day of walking or making.
To return to music, or to read the starred dark dawn-blind.

Half Dead

Half dead with tiredness, wakened quick at night
With dysentry pangs, going blind among sleepers
And dazed into half dark — illness had its spite.
My head cleared; and the horrible body-creepers
Stilled with the cold — the cold bringing me sane —
See there was Witcombe Steep as it were, but no beeches there
And the clear flames of stars over the crest bare
Mysterious showing on the dim cloths of heaven,
Hanging majestic mild folds, gray blue (gold-fretted) even
Along the East sky far deep in full March, Her night.
Dark was the famed Mausoleum after that sight.

Today

The unclean hells and the different Hell's terrors
That seized the heart — O! but the black death should
With pure touch end this tangle of wild errors,
And numb the sense again to the nerve and the blood.
Generations have known fear, it is written in the books.
Men turned wry-souled with tortures beyond men —
Dreadful are the morning heavens in their lovely looks
Mocking the hope of shaping earth's thought again,
For men deny honour as of the spirit of their blood,
And it is I, a war-poet, mark of the greed of evil mood,
Whose right is of earth's requirings of Man, honour and gratitude.

Early Spring Dawn

Long shines the thin light of the day to north-east,
The line of blue faint known and the leaping to white
The meadows lighten, mists lessen, but light is increased,
The sun soon will appear, and dance, leaping with light.

Now milkers hear faint through dreams first cockerel make crow,
Faint yet arousing thought, soon must the milk pails be flowing
Gone out the level sheets of mists, and the West row
Of elms are black on the meadow edge, Day's dear wind is blowing.

First Time In

After the dread tales and red yarns of the Line
Anything might have come to us; but the divine
Afterglow brought us up to a Welsh colony
Hiding in sandbag ditches, whispering consolatory
Soft foreign things. Then we were taken in
To low huts candle-lit shaded close by slitten
Oilsheets, and there but boys gave us kind welcome;
So that we looked out as from the edge of home.
Sang us Welsh things, and changed all former notions
To human hopeful things. And the next days' guns
Nor any Line-pangs ever quite could blot out
That strangely beautiful entry to War's rout,
Candles they gave us precious and shared over-rations —
Ulysses found little more in his wanderings without doubt.
'David of the White Rock', the 'Slumber Song' so soft, and that
Beautiful tune to which roguish words by Welsh pit boys
Are sung — but never more beautiful than here under the guns'
    noise.

Cotswold

Cotswold Edge shines out at morning in gold,
It convinces as Rome convinces in the earth-stronghold
The traveller finds here and there in his walk and is sure
Of the might of her of Rome, and her right to endure.
But Cotswold Wall stands up and has strength of its own,
Blue against dawn, Sunset's shield, and Time's wonder and crown.
And Crickley unconscious so strong She is in Her pride,
Is master of meadows away to far Severn side —
And no man says Her nay, She is a County's wonder:
That County, Gloucestershire, wherefore many have crossed seas
    and died —
At Laventie I saw them, and at Ypres in the cannon thunder,
Rome would have kept silence at such courage not praised — Her
    own beside.

The Song

A Country ignorant of its own songs,
Of that which nearest and most to it belongs:
The true talk of the soil, the current with its sky,
The remembrancer of all keenness of memory.
Men go soldiering across strange tideways
Risk death on strange soils, slide on unfamiliar clays,
Their battle songs shreds of clown's breakdown tricks;
Town refuse . . . while the ardours and rattle-of-sticks
Of 'High Germany', or 'I'm only Ninety-Eight',
Stay in the books, a dry antiquarian fate,
They go to desperate chances with mean songs, and go straight.

At Bourton or Rissington one heard, 'Widdicombe Fair',
Story and string of names set to a free jolly air;
While Rouen or Buire-au-Bois sang Mile End's-Holloway's favourite
Drolleries, and the Line was pleased with Plumstead's delight.
Precious candle light lit vast in the wide barn
On soldiers, farmers' sons, wakers at first morn,
Dawn's lovers; losing separateness in orts of cheap wit,
Tomorrow might go under for an ill-written chit —
Now snatched by music high above body's cares;
Be frightened, washed darkly over by wind-bundled flares;
Such tiredness and endurance, pleased by such airs!
But I sang 'The Blacksmith's Song' on march near Estaires,
And 'Farmer's Boy' made free body by Chelmsford — dusky tillers.

La Gorgues

The long night, the short sleep, and La Gorgues to wander,
So be the Fates were kind and our Commander;
With a mill, and still canal, and like-Stroudway bridges.
One looks back on these as Time's truest riches —
Which were so short an escape, so perilous a joy —
Since fatigues, weather, Line trouble, or any whimsical play
Division might hatch out would have finished peace.

There was a house there — (I tell the most noted thing)
The kindest woman kept, and an unending string
Of privates as wasps to sugar went in and out.
Friendliness sanctified all there without doubt,
As lovely as the brick mill above the still green
Canal where the dark fishes went almost unseen.
Gloucester's B Company had come down from Tilleloy, they
Lousy, thirsty, avid of any employ

Of peace; and this woman in leanest times had plotted
A miracle to amaze the army-witted — the time-cheated.
And this was café-au-lait as princes know it:
And fasting, and poor-struck; dead but not so as to show it,
A drink of epics, dooms, battles, a height of tales,
Rest, heat, cream, coffee; the maker tries and fails
The poet too, where such need such satisfaction had,
A campaign thing that makes keen remembrance sad.

It was light there, too, in the clear North French way,
It blessed the room and bread; and the mistress-giver . . .
The husband for his wife's sake, both for more than a day
Were blessed by many soldiers tired however, and forever
A mark in Time, a Peace, a Making-delay.
God bless the honourers of boy soldiers and the folk generous
Who dwell in light clean houses, and are glad to be thus
Serving France with love generous, in the light, clean house.

Northleach

Northleach, that jewel, white stone and green foliage,
Breadth in the street walk, dignity in dwelling,
On the Roman way standing. That jewel of Cotswold no love's sign
     wanting
But of the remembrance most there stays now, hot tea
Taken early of morning after sleeping in a barn,
Got by importunacy, given me by courtesy.
(And kind faces) which should alone be a white tower
From Elizabeth Her time — standing to praise Drayton's hour.
But the body, as the spirit, demands natural poetry
Tea on the high Cotswolds — at an Inn, noble from the wealth of
     corn.

Clouds Die Out In June

Clouds die out in June where the sun drops —
The skies are clear as water when the sand stops
In flood time, settles; and the winds have settled now.
Stars as bright sand grains remain, and the still flow
Of the high heavens like deep sea water not hides
Them, as the course of the Heavens nobly, strongly glides.
There are the hours' tides, the sky's and the Eternal tides
Over the dark day's tides.
But for all my worship of these, I shall go in to studies
Of music or verse or Elizabethans — in my labour's plans,
See lamp light — make notes and verse — read noble words
     sufficient
Only to come out when the thought will not move to its bent.
Longford dark worshipping upwards to the dim sky
I dazed a little, till walking, moving easily and lonelily
I came to the brook meadow with its line of elm trees,
The small bridge that has dignity and its own heart's place,
To turn there, and be glad that night wide is come
All men asleep save I, in my loved-never so loved town,
And my friends asleep; while I work and my honour and clear eyes
     keep
Waiting for the dawn as first mark — and more clouds of high June.

Blighty

It seemed that it were well to kiss first earth
On landing, having traversed the narrow seas,
And grasp so little, tenderly, of this field of birth.
France having trodden and lain on, travelled bending the knees.
And having shed blood — known heart for Her and last nerve freeze,
Proved body past heart, and soul past (so we thought) any worth
For what so dear a thing as the first homecoming,
The seeing smoke pillar aloft from the home dwellings;
Sign of travel ended, lifted awhile the dooming
Sentence of exile; homecoming, right of tale-tellings.
But mud is on our fate after so long acquaintance,
We find of England the first gate without Romance;
Blue paved wharfs with dock-policemen and civic decency,
Trains and restrictions, order and politeness and directions,
Motion by black and white, guided ever about ways
And staleness with petrol-dust distinguishing days.
A grim faced black-garbed mother efficient and busy
Set upon housework, worn-minded and fantasy free —
A work-house matron, forgetting Her old birth friend — the Sea.

The Bargain

For two grains of wheat grown on Waltheof's field
To the abbot of Stare, the Mill of Knuts Weald
Should be to Waltheof he and heirs for ever.
Nine hundred years passed, and the weir baulked endeavour,
Water banked up in the old February manner,
Though never Hugo passed there with bright banner.
Now Waltheof's field grew no more lovely grain,
A brick kiln stood there and blazed at the clay's pain,

Rubbish heaped there and waste paper wind scattered,
Two grains of wheat were all ever that mattered.
What easier thing than to sow a handful of corn?
Scratched earth in Spring, a scatter, and stalks were born
From the waste, the weedy corner of side's path.
Tenure held, money was made there and the field felt death
Sinking deeper, the bowels of it taken far
To be villas, schools, churches freaked perpendicular
And lovely soil made rough square; money bringing
Saleable bricks. Water came, the black moorhens flinging
Frightened courses, reeds sedges stood up in small woods,
The last island of clay vanished, and lonelier moods
Possessed the pit now, mere and most melancholy.
Town Council had no poetry and decided ceremoniously
That the rubbish there (surely) as elsewhere might be voided.
(Five pounds a year and two grains wheat was cheap,)
Waltheof's field will become a rubbish heap,
Villas will stand there and look polite — with folk polite
Where sedges stood for the wind's play and poet-delight,
But Severn will be sorry and it can never be right.

Laventie Ridge

The low ridge of Laventie
Looked like Wainlode's
Coming up from Sandhurst's
Orchard guarded roads.

And the stars above the ridge
Were nearly as those
Glowing by Maisemore bridge
Where the weir-fall goes.

To guard me homeward
To dear friends of mine,
Kisses gave me music
And Bach better than starshine.

But Aubers knew my musing
And the Preludes with
Thoughts of a dear one homeward
With stars mingled in love.

Sheer Falls of Green Slope

Sheer falls of green slope against setting sun
And ruled by high majestic Severn vapour —
These are not easily known, when talking is done;
Life's truth fades awfully set down on plain paper
When Cotswold or the Severn-land's in question
And the maker must do — before the poem is done or known.
Here as of Aeschylus or Sophocles the reading
Square Greek things thrust from thought and brought to that height
By happy or strong men wrought to a known master thing
Rough with no thought of small pains, wrestling not minding of
    bleeding.

So Crickley stands with Homer's clouds high over, high over,
So Birdlip rises sheer on her north steep —
The old vineyard falls at one leap
And the deep
Villa-land is sheltered and sure in sleep,
And sentinels, patricians and Roman farmers and their dear women
Return to where the willow herb for September their true colour
    keep.

The Essential Things

Fire and water makes a home's centre
And lamplight fills the heart of a room,
The year goes round from summer to winter
With shades of dark light and varying gloom.

For brown tea these two things are managed
And mixed for rest or further action,
Summer with soft light or Winter with plain etched
Branches, fire and water minister to satisfaction.

If Ben Jonson Were Back

If Ben Jonson he were back what strong things then
Should take the ears both and eyes of common men!
What draught of the huge City where night signs blink
Above Waterloo's bridge on the river's dark brink,
Where he warehouses saw, and the wingéd tall ships
That now stay eastward by Poplar and Limehouse steam crane tips.
What pictures of the crowd no pen can draw
Save his, who could command the complete show
Of Smithfield or the inn rooms of Westminster;
Who drew bow in Tothill — and had in Flanders no fear.
Fleet, Southwark, Paul's; and the light fopling knew
The shopmen, knaves, gulls and drank with apprentices.
While to-day the poets have polite friends and family circles
And say the right things and go early and polite to bed,
Never talk of Elizabethans — nor drink wine red
Nor glory in great talk till the dawn makes new glory shown.
They follow not his ways, and they live half-dead.
If Ben Jonson were back he would teach them human

Ways and words — not to sin so against God and the common
Delights of man — work, talk, rest and the morning star breaking
   over the guest.

Tewkesbury

Tewkesbury, that square thing, name of stone and battle,
Where all things come, the Western men and cattle,
Scatter the environ dust and wish for Thee
Out beyond Forthampton or towards Ledbury.
Danes have made havoc there, Normans piled memorial;
Stow's wool in baleful grew to a white-brown stock there,
Evesham grew plums from blossom to a hope of wealth there;
Apples she sent, and mustard blared strong in a tilth there;
Stow's new morrice was looked for soon and plays under the moon,
Stratford's gossip made Lucy there, Justice and Knight — a loon.
Tavern on tavern lit ruddy in gloom of richness.
The watchers that worried their hearts of Gloucester's near doom
And got the last short word out of carter or groom.
North, South, East, West run the roads predestined and
Shall so run while England for memory and love shall yet stand
Or Cotswold Roman looks to Briton Malvern so grand.

Old Tale

If one's heart is broken twenty times a day,
What easier thing to fling the bits away,
But still one gathers fragments, and looks for wire
Or patches it up like some old bicycle tyre.

Bicycle tyres fare hardly on roads, but the heart
Has an easier time than rubber; they sheath a cart
With iron, I'll sheathe my own — my mind must be made
To bother the heart, and to teach things, and learn it its trade.

Thoughts on Beethoven

Beethoven I wronged thee undernoting thus
Thy dignity and worth; the overplus
Of one quartett would our book overweigh
Who see not the gold star dying out nobly from day.
You have our great Ben's mastery and a freer
Carriage of method, spice of the open air,
Which he our greatest builder had not so;
Not as his own at least, but acquiréd-to.
Your eyes saw Dawn and spirits and mists withdraw,
His talking men, friends parted by dawn to take
Way by Thames till the few hours of sleep were known
But he with you kept watch with Homer, heart awake.
Only the worshipper's spirit was truly yours
His the great labourer from dusk till dawn indoors.
Homer, Ben Jonson, Shakespeare and a pillar of us,
Friends, talkers and walkers, and immortal great doers
Such are our memories which false betray
The thought of daylight even in minds gray.

And even Rasoumoffsky to a lighter fame
Forget for a while — with its Greek strengths and worshipping
    flame,
Till Ben Jonson gave my mind pride — and to your might my
    homage came.

Small Chubby Dams

Small chubby dams banked in the water
Flowing half as clear quite as the soft air,
Going placid westward, a small daughter
Between Crickley and Severn, and only there.
Short childhood, early youth, but dead primal fires
Set limits to a flowing thing's girl's desires.
The one thing was to live that short course sprackly;
Therefore nuthazels and ashes hanging all slackly
Regarding boughs, he drew to familiar plants round him
As foxgloves dusty purple with serrate rim
And willow herb and lady's mantle and dark flower dim
A hundred dainty watchers of clear eddies
Ladies of common soil, and fine mould ladies;
To perfect himself, and comfort one such as I;
Too ill for walking plans, left but to try the uplifted
The instant medicine of the smooth sky.
Chancing on this (not written) as shapely Slow Movement as
Brahms he made ever, but native to more grace.

Poets

Who would have thought the men that watched the stars
Move to their dawn places without jars
And freezing their being to them of death's nights —
And held their being to them for Heaven's high lights,
(Soul and body and mind hanging on to Eridanus kind,)
Would so tamely on common custom followed
And lain all the unsurpassed night of hours in the hollowed
Shameful warm sheets and wool; so easy policed were they!
A hundred poets stood to welcome in day
In a Company's front, that's dawn's love and stir and tea.
A hundred of them: some lived, some were put past wonder
With pain, others died in dreadfullest brute thunder,
Some lived, but since the police will always make question
Landladies enquire, and neighbours offer any suggestion —
Since life is life and bedtime bedtime, then these
Accept also the immemorial tame set decrees
Of bed-and-breakfast, office and life by degrees.
But one Ben Jonson honoured, and took at dawn his verses
In London City — to meet dawn and tea-drinking apprentices:
And take at resting his verses over tea, both virtues tasting.

June's Meadows

Swathes laid breaker like in long shore waves,
And gleaming with dew's fall of the middle night,
Nine o'clock mix of dark and sunny glories,
(The clouds moved so — light so caresses and loves).
These are the stuff of poems, of these I would write,
But to hang on that theme, fitting music or stories,
Tales that a town living folk looks over and craves
For days golden again, for the Golden Age.

Roofed over with clouds continual of varying rage,
Rage of shape, colour, or ranked confident line.
Such tales might bring wonder to men, and that
Growing to action, should the will create
For eager shaping to what Time may divine, make divine.
But that's a strength in story denied to me,
So hide the thought close unless the lure may be
Keen on the spirit as myself (or other) and he
Search out the needed; the local one, the antiquary,
He play literary ghost to my labouring all loving pen
To be a good remembrancer to men in this Valley again.

Roads — Those Roads

Roads are sometimes the true symbolical
Representations of movement in the fate of man.
One goes from Severn of tales and sees Wales
A wall against England as since time began.

Hawthorn and poplar call to mind the different people
That ruled and had shaping of this land at their periods.
One goes from the Abbey to the smaller steeples,
There made worthy, and by tithe-barns, and all by roads.

Daylight colours gray them, they are stained blue by the April
Skies on their pools and Summer makes carpet of dust
Fit for the royal; Autumn smothers all with colour
Blown clean away by the withering cruel Winter's gust.

Roads are home-coming and a hope of desire reached,
(There is the orange window at the curve of the dark way),
Whether by Winter white frozen or by Summer bleached,
Roads are the right pride of man and his anxiety.

Prelude (12/8 Time)

The gaiety of colours
Of the school groups
Going at midday
To onions or soups,
Is all one with June
And the flooding meadows,
Meadowsweet, sorrel
And the sable shadows.

White roads are blinding
In the full heat,
They shade their eyes
And pass discreet —
The stranger wondering
With rested delight
At their casualness and discreteness
And cottage clothes bright.

Deerhurst Church

There is something wrong there, with that the gracefullest
Of strong things Severn knows and had long loved best,
A tall thing clean and poised like any boy walker
Above where the swamp dwellings and old fastnesses were,
Such reeds and broad stretches recall inevitably
The otter hunter and wild heron stalker
Gone whole day in the chase, and the flat boats, and glee
Of Saxon children the bright bream or lank eel to see.
The business of wood managing, ploughing or of seam caulker
The one manor held of war-service in fee —

Entry in Domesday Book; and a whimsy of yearly
Performance. People come there yet for the old chapel
Found at haphazard, the Saxon thing, and a famous;
Where this thing is — dear *Lavengro* recalling thus —
Come upon where loneliness lies and our poplars dapple
In their long frame of shadow strong meadows tremulous.
There is something wrong, but right things not so often are
All just in their perfection; as in disappointing.
This upright unexpected white shell of stone —
Save few cottages — in the water meadow alone.
Whether one's surprised admiration does dare
To ask more than in Gloucestershire the eyes let known;
Or if the desire is never shaming or daunting.

Lovely Playthings

Dawn brings lovely playthings to the mind
But sunset fights and goes down in battle blind;
The banners of dawn spread over in mystery,
But nightfall ends a boast and a pageantry.

After the halt of dawn comes the slow moving of
Time, till the sun's hidden rush and the day is admitted;
Sunset dies out in a smother of something like love
With dew and the elm-hung stars, and owl outcries half-witted.

Late May

Dawn comes queerly in late May
With dim north light all night. It grows unlooked for, all at once
The light is perceived to increase, and a wind stirs . . . . .
One worships the stars for the last time, and thinks of the day;
Rising from under dark beech or feathery firs
With a stiffness and soreness of feet and coldness of bones
And stumbles in dark for the gate and the sight of roadway.
To get the blood warm — and the thought moving like blood.
To think of Helen in the North, and the worships by the Forth
Or Hebrides — and what Midsummer Night knew of beautiful
Ceremonial, all clean worded, and lovely-natural.
Going down Portway to the far lights of guessed at Gloucester —
Where tea waits, and books, dreams of perceived slopes of hill.
And perhaps a music to make of the worship of the North.

Songs Come To The Mind

Songs come to the mind —
Other men's songs
Or one's own, when something is kind
And remembers not any wrongs.

Swift cleaving paths in air
On a bicycle, or slow
Wandering and wondering where
One's purposes may go.

Songs come and are taken, written,
Snatched from the momentary
Accidents of light, shape, spirit meeting
For one light second spirit, unbelievably.

Dawn

To see the dawn soak darkness, look out now,
Open window, smell the air, and be happy though
The day but one acted routine is known —
Not walking or mere living in warmth of the sun;
Moving, pacing by him till the day is done
And a new necessity of argument is travelled to . . .
Look out now, see azure through the crystal air;
And pink flares, pretty or feathery small clouds there
Above the unrisen light so glorious boasting.
And with the pride of a poet, praise the Maker's pride —
Who imagined so, and to night workers gives easy-paid
Wonders and understandings of natural delight.
To lie down for one hour, or drink tea and to go on,
Watching the different tremendous or familiar majesties
Of my friend — and my advocate with God — the Sun,
Whom none loved yet more — not my Master, the great Ben Jonson.

Buysscheure

Many times I have seen windmills, or grassy slopes
Framed black against soft cloud on the ridges' tops
But Buysscheure's mill that might have whirled a hundred years
Stays in my mind with like strolling and comrade Gloucesters,
And my poet hopes out there; and musician's hopes.
And there was St. Omer later, golden in the hollow —
Noble as French towns are, I could imagine the follow
Of red tiled house on red-tiled house by the canal,
Lovely black smoke rising golden in the proud sunfall.
St. Omer, loved of generations of lovers and citizens
Like Dutch to me; and poetic with rich unfamiliar

Beauty and order, and ruddy tiling friend to clear air.
There was straw and good billets and eatables of small cost,
But of Buysscheure, the mill and St. Omer I remember most.

The Poet Walking

I saw people
Thronging the streets
Where the Eastway with the old
Roman Wall meets —
But none though of old
Gloucester blood brought,
Loved so the City
As I — the poet unthought.
And I exulted there
To think that but one
Of all that City
Had pride or equity
Enough for the marvelling
At street and stone,
Or the age of Briton,
Dane, Roman, Elizabethan —
One grateful one — true child of that dear City — one worthy one.

The Comparison

What Malvern is the day is, and its touchstone
Gray velvet, or moonmarked; rich, or bare as bone;
One looks toward Malvern and is tuned to the whole,
The world swings round him, as the Bear to the Pole.

Men have crossed seas to know how Paul's tops Fleet;
So music has wrapt them high in the mere street
While none or few will care how the curved giants stand,
(Those strengths upthrust!) on the meadow and plough-land.

But God wondered, when Wren heaved up Dome above Thames,
Worcestershire to Herefordshire Beacon learnt shapes and different
     names.
He is a Wonderer still, though men grow cold and chill —
And walk accustomed by Staunton or up Ludgate Hill.

Strange Hells

There are strange Hells within the minds War made
Not so often, not so humiliatingly afraid
As one would have expected — the racket and fear guns made.
One Hell the Gloucester soldiers they quite put out;
Their first bombardment, when in combined black shout
Of fury, guns aligned, they ducked lower their heads
And sang with diaphragms fixed beyond all dreads,
That tin and stretched-wire tinkle, that blither of tune;
'Après la guerre fini' till Hell all had come down.
12 inch — 6 inch and 18 pounders hammering Hell's thunders.

Where are they now on State-doles, or showing shop-patterns
Or walking town to town sore in borrowed tatterns
Or begged. Some civic routine one never learns.
The heart burns — but has to keep out of face how heart burns.

Crickley Morning

Morning struck the first steel of cloud light,
And steel and armour changed to flooding oceans
Of light, with infinite slow cautions and motions;
Full power awaiting and signals of full delight.
Faded away strength to sea-shells of fashion exquisite;
Delicate; to tiny sea-shell trinkets of waves
Touched with unmatched separate pallors of light;
Rose-coloured, ocean matching; the last spirit to delight of music.

But there was coffee to my body's need,
And fire had to be made — and of music a screed.
There was Dryhill meadow to calm the thought to birth,
And there were books of familiar and heart-precious earth.
So put aside the matchless glories, for those who were more
Worthy, or loved not earth or writing as I did — to the door
Of the small cottage going in — to work out thoughts of musing
By the Camp — or the pine wood — or the marsh; pen and ink to
     find the mood.

Memory

Shepherd's warning, and all too gay forerunning
Action of day, and sense of boastfulness
And a sense of unsureness; the high sky dunning
With cloud, and the willow sober in July dress . . . .
Yet Cotswold's edge may pull the new day together,
That's but a fool yet, and has fool's wantonness.
With mist and falsity of colour, refusal of beauty,
And She of all England's Company a high Princess.
But whether shepherd shall take the warning, shall not I
The ploughfield that loves me shall feel my feet — wet or dry.
I shall be in Sandhurst meadows before the sun is most high.
Gloucester — though — this is less than your pleasure, surely less.

That Centre of Old

Is it only Cotswold that holds the glamour
Memory felt of England in the gun-stammer —
Thud, smack, belch of war — and kept virtue by?
I do not know, but only that most unhappy,
The hills are to me what to happy I
They were in Somme muckage baths and east of Laventie
When hunger made one worthy to absorb the sky —
Look, or play fancy-tricks with small cloudlets high.
Count them — or dare not count — love and let go by.
Now as ever Cotswold rewards the mere being and seeing
As truly as
Ever in the relief of knowing mere being
In the still space
At a strafe end grateful for silence and body's grace.
(Whole body — and after Hell's hammering and clamouring.)

Then memory purified made rewarding shapes
Of all that spirit runs towards in escapes
And Cooper's Hill showed plain almost as experience.
Soft winter mornings of kind innocence, high June's
Girls' air of untouched purity and on Cooper's Hill
Or Autumn Cranham with its boom of colour . . .
Not anyway does ever Cotswold's fail — Her dear blue long dark
    slope fail
Of the imagining promise in full exile.

Incredible Thing

The mutineers, true Romans that once were Scyllas
Had never dreamed of bijou or neat villas.
Clear marching minds; but we are threatened with worse
Profanation, on Man's longing a bitterer curse.

To guard for foes with a hundred years of toil
Is an accepted bargain, but the sea's low soil
Itself may be piled to cirrus for a fool's whim,
Titus or Galba had never heard of such as him.

There are those that will not praise God with gratitude
Whose strength to cruelty stoops and the foolishest mood
Who'd strike the sky for bravado, and blind out the stars
But take no danger — keep clear of the hazard of dim wars.

Up Horsepools

Ford that I could not read, but spent miles of road on,
They say was melancholy, but that fineness shows
Through the plainness. He was one of them and his stars
The true London Stars. Whether health, or some unforgotten
Grief spoilt achievement I cannot say: only — only
The high white road and green deep valleys there lonely
And his flatness would not agree; the mild air pure
Spoilt his grave virtue — of town that; he numbed so there
Clearness of eye, freshness of mind; Roman virtue showed
White stretch of road leading up to high Cotswold.
All reading in patience; but Ford nearly worst was known
Of all Gloriana's great writers of fine renown.
Because the Mermaid print after familiar Morley
Was ugly — and the bad plays spoilt the good ones surely.
Standing by Marston, Greene and Shirley's so chaste
Words, that all evil forbade, spoke out clearly, stood fast.

Crickley

Crickley makes clouds to gather there
For the glory of him; the cliffs that golden as Greece
Give back the glories of vapour of middle air.
Hugy rounded giants of smooth limbed slack kneed peace;
Atlantic wonderful unconscious Titans bare.
Crickley gathers conies, starlings and lonely kites,
Grass snakes and butterflies, and of lucent nights
A host of milky stars with rich light astare,
(Virgil and Catullus runs soft in the sentry's mind there).
Crickley has gray common and streaked plough
Young water dances there for the joy of birth.

Scabious, willow herb and great tansy stand now —
There is everything there that shows common love of earth
And Roman, Roman from dawn shows to last sunset flare,
Not challenging — not She of Asia, but of Mantuan earth.

There dawn, rounding the north, strikes dimness through —
A wind stirs tremulous about the leaves, and shows
Curves like any carved thing, or of life that goes;
Gray changes through the later grays to light blue.
There the shepherd comes among the morning mists
His flock crops grass unprofitable enough;
The hill-slopes herbage dry enough, brittle and gray-rough,
Long ago rabbits ran on their maze of twists;
Long ago song woke of welcome near the coppice nests.
Roman is Crickley, the mail clangs and shines there.
Morning broadens, the valley reveals dark lines,
Shurdington bars the first sun out with avenues of pines,
Malvern shows royalty, one has the earth spaces;
Gone up in transparency are the drifting light hazes.

Crickley gathers the day's full forces there
Bronze and soft dreaming gold and blue steel out of air,
And Roman are the slopes for all the ploughman,
Or Briton, or after Dane-master since time began.
Their guessed-at ways and talk in the night camps
Comparison of Cotswolds with the Companion Lamps
And the eternal heart grumbling of the dear exile
Whose blood to whose earth yearns — and will deny to be still.
Sun swings his course above her, but in no more
Majestic line than his curve as steady as sure
Southward, to fir trees musical, and quiet beech trees.
Cliffs as if carved ready for great inscription
(Of Cirencester or Gloucester cohort of Legion),
Sheer up down, where the magpies live and the run
Of happy rabbits till day closes is never done.
(On afternoons I think the garrison dozes,

Romans of Constantine's time) and beneath wild roses;
Hemlock, willow herb, scabious, keep as long untoucht
As ever anywhere with stray sheep-wool clutcht
On bitter, lovely sprays, and bee orchises grow.
They touched them, the Romans, with such love as I with such
    memories,
On the Roman slopes such brambles their long cloaks snatched.
Afternoon passes, tea time comes, wood-smoke rises,
Evening comes on with sea-sting on her dark breezes
Orange blinds shine, stars show, and the round of sky
Falls to the Severn. Making comes after that clarity
Of exact truth; coolness and close wrapping dim lucency
Of vast breathing gray shades — night's foregoing majesty.

Then how he is large and calm. How still with the stars!
(Beethoven alone tells his truth — still after watchings and wars.)
How self-sufficient, how great with his slopes and scars!
What silence save the weird cries of the lone owl!
Cutting like steel the dark sweep of the wide whole
Hollow of edge, and all starry air-tide there.
Crickley, of all small hills ever that were,
You are the prince of them, wholly without peer,
And have the Briton and Dane, but the strict Roman honour.

The Fatigue Party

Not a thing to see, pitch black-misty rainy night
With Verey lights confusing to helpless spite —
Men that must for two miles somehow get heaved
Rations in sandbags, through such mud would have cleaved
To Leviathan himself, and unshorn noble Samson.
Four black hours before the thing get done and we lie down.
Slippery duckboards and shell holes, and continual, continual
Mudsmears — swears and shoulders hurt with the strings —
Shoulders hurt with cuts and the sandbag weightings.
How to get there? How could human beings ever get there?
It was done — with heart's blood. The heart took treble strains and
    over
And yet stood. We were finished, our souls urged us. Heart stood
And after dumping the things, with shoulders lighter than air
Across that vile land, in the vile night unfit for the human,
We struggled and at last turned an oil sheet and saw glimmer
Felt warmth, lay down to think of Cotswold, some loved boy or
    woman
(The friend who drew my heart out to the heart of Beethoven).

Bacon of Mornings

To the West Country dawn comes with crystal breath,
But there to crackles and sweet smell of bacon;
Men cleaned rifles to conceal desire beneath,
Or nobly kept still fortitude silent unshaken
With maxims from the other (Shakespeare) Bacon —
The mixed thoughts of another day awaken
Of by Bourton or Stow or the Slaughters — but not these slaughters
Of death after months' fear — horrible to see. But by happy waters

Running (I know not) to Colne, or Chelt, Thames or Severn,
While here the slow Lys is miles off — Somme, seventy and seven
(Not that we wished to see Somme river of evil fame).
Dawn was sweet here also, bringing tea and letters, papers —
And the new hunger for tobacco — and friends talk of comfortable
Home things, and of other friends — thought of snowy white table;
Which they, hours not up yet — would arrange neatly and share
Bread in loaves and butter, and true jam in pots there,
Bacon not put in tins, but Christianly made to prepare.
And the *Daily Mail* to give them the news that we —
In the devil of it — could neither make guess at nor see.
Here dawn and tea and rest was comfort, comfort.
And the letters up, and to dodge breakfast and keep bread's part.
But though one might read Chapman here there were shopkeepers
    there
Who could not give such glory, but a job and living wage clear,
And as for Ben Jonson — he was friend of night workers
Better in Gloucestershire rooms in candle light's brights and glooms
Than in dark dugout at night wasting hours — unwilling shirkers.

The Soaking

The rain has come, and the earth must be very glad
Of its moisture, and the made roads all dust-clad —
It lets a veil down on the lucent dark
And not of any bright ground thing shows any its spark.

Tomorrow's gray morning will show cow-parsley
Hung all with shining drops, and the river will be
Duller because of the all unfamiliar soddenness of things,
Till the skylark breaks his reluctance, hangs shaking and sings.

Merville

The whitest thing in life save Gloucester's tall
Tower, was Merville's, at Toussaints at the leaves' fall.
Across cabbages, others and unending lettuces,
Bathed lucent in October calm-touching breezes,
Wide-stretching; and the poplars colouring strawn roads.
The whitest thing. The tall tower there in the sky!

They say it is fallen since (O North!) but sure am I
No lover of standing signs of up-shaped stone piles
Will forget that church, and the flat land's gathering smiles.
Gone the shrine, I suppose, but some man will recall
How shrines looked and this, perhaps, the gravest of all.
One looked, passed, walked the curve and saw sudden as pain
Merville lucent in the wide light, as after soft rain
Most towers; most high things seem; and pack or sore feet
Right hand or left hand file, one must joggle one's straps
And not into mere suffering private for a moment relapse.
O, to be on Ludgate Hill, or Gloucester City — Her great street.
Not till the third halt, Merville or such beauties seem
Possible to the mind — or far Gloucester hidden lovely in the dream.

New Year's Eve

Aveluy and New Year's Eve, and the time as tender
As if green buds grew. In the low West a slender
Streak of last orange. Guns mostly deadest still
And a noise of limbers near coming down the hill.
Nothing doing, nothing doing, and a screed to write;
Candles enough for books, a sleepy delight
In the warm dugout, day ended, nine hours to the light.

There now and then now, one nestled down snug,
A head is enough to read by, and cover up with a rug.

Electric! Clarinet sang of a Hundred Pipers
And hush awe mystery vanished like tapers
Of tobacco smoke, there was great hilarity then!
Breath and a queer tube magicked sorrow from men.

And the North with Sir Walter and Burns and lovely wide humanity
Was clear as by Perthshire, or Ayrshire — or Forth going to sea.
How keep the blankets — how *Spirit of Man* or Borrow to read?
Music fired the heart till the blood found thought and said
No more than 'A Hundred Pipers' could I keep to bed.

Robecq — A Memory

Robecq that's swept away now, so men tell
Is but the faintest hint of what once was well;
Memory to fact — but a savour still a light taste
Stays as a phantom and holds, clinging there fast
As a thought of skies, a girl's way, or an inn's shelter —
Poplars' strewn leaves down wind gone helter skelter.
Gone; October's farewell sweet in first frost;
Far Merville glimmering far like faint milky ghost
Are as worth remembrance as the unthought broken welter
Of Ypres or wide Albert in high day.
Black time takes much and hides these things away,
But Robecq is prayer to my soul, for the thought of Merville's tower
And I cannot pretend tears to what my soul dreads to have die.

Possessions

France has Victory, England yet firm shall stay,
But what shall please the wind now the trees are away
War took on Witcombe steep?
It breathes there, and wonders at old roarings
October time at all lights; and the new clearings
For memory are like to weep.
War need not cut down trees, three hundred miles over Seas
Children of those the Romans saw — lovely trunk and great sail trees!
Not on Cranham, not on Cooper's of camps;
Friend to the great October stars — and the July sky lamps.

Billet

O, but the racked clear tired strained frames we had!
Tumbling in the new billet on to straw bed,
Dead asleep in eye shutting. Waking as sudden
To a golden and azure room, a golden racheted
Lovely web of blue seen and blue shut, and cobwebs and tiles,
And gray wood dusty with time. June's girlish kindest smiles.
Rest at last and no danger for another week, a seven-day week.
But one Private took on himself a Company's heart to speak,
'I wish to bloody Hell I was just going to Brewery — surely
To work all day (in Stroud) and be free at tea-time — allowed
Resting when one wanted, and a joke in season,
To change clothes and take a girl to Horsepool's turning,
Or drink a pint at "Traveller's Rest", and find no cloud.
Then God and man and war and Gloucestershire would have a
     reason,
But I get no good in France, getting killed, cleaning off mud.'
He spoke the heart of all of us — the hidden thought burning,
     unturning.

Rouen

I am not jealous of any town for Gloucester
Save Rouen, with its great rock and blue swift waterway,
Streets which were first shown to me in the Studio
At Charing Cross, where books take City air all day.
And the pines there, by the drill ground, where by Yea and Nay
English and dazed recruits drilled for endless hours;
The Balzac statue, bridges, and two soaring towers
To seaward aloft ever looking far as for Nelson away
After the afterglow so clear like Gloucester own;
But briefer, the wise sober high conceivéd town.
Two books also I owe to the City of Rouen,
Le Curé de Tours and another — both loved as of my own
Country — and the lion like tawny rock challenging the plain and the
    sun.

Glimmering Dusk

Glimmering dusk above the moist plough and the
Silence of trees' heaviness under low gray sky
Are some comfort for the mind gone soft in lethargy,
White road dark with pools, but growing soon to dry;
But the mind complains, 'This indeed is beauty enough
And comfort, but itself not enough cure for sorrows,
Nor equal weight for good things, and fine stuff
Of thought snatched ruthlessly by thieves best under harrows.'
But the soul would not be denied; comfort from the night
Gathered, the mind unwilling, hope past all thought of matters
Of right anger — and the body only spoke of its plight
That a kind law makes dust of at last and scatters,
No notice the soul took — it desired God with all friendly might
The leaves not sodden moved on trees with winter patters.

Friendly Are Meadows

Friendly are meadows when the sun's gone down in
And no bright colour spoils the broad green of gray,
And one's eyes rest looking to Cotswold away, the northline away,
Under cloud ceilings whorled, and most largely fashioned
With seventeenth century curves of the tombstone way —
A day of softnesses, of comfort of no false din.
Sorrel makes rusty rest for thy eyes, and the worn path
Brave elms, and stiles, willows by dyked water-run
North-France general look, and a sort of bath
Of freshness — a light wrap of comfortableness
Over one's being, a sense of strings music begun —
A slow gradual symphony of worthiness —
Quartetts dreamed of perfection achieved masterless,
As by Robecq I dreamed them, and to Estaires gone.
But this is Cotswold, Severn; when these go stale
The universal and wide decree shall fail —
England, Her natural love shall fall to be
The admirer of the strange false thing — the freak of beauty
Or strength — a rainbow or eclipse — or lightning riven tree,
And Elizabethans be no more remembered for plain truth and glory

Loam Lies Heavy

Loam lies heavy on the lightless flesh
And clay's a heavy thing, and wards off decay;
But sand is light and chance might scatter away
To leave the bare bone unhidden to change afresh.
Sunlight would search it, rain make clammy, and dew
Shiningness, the ants or other creatures explore
First fissures, the thing would become human no more,

Nothing to that which loved to walk wide fields through,
Nothing to that which moved in the high June woods midnight dew,
Or loved Christmas ceremonial on high Rome's Camps frore.

Crucifix Corner

There was a water dump there, and regimental
Carts came every day to line up and fill full
Those rolling tanks with chlorinated clear mixture;
And curse the mud with vain veritable vexture.
Aveluy across the valley, billets, shacks, ruins,
With time and time a crump there to mark doings.
On New Year's Eve the marsh glowed tremulous
With rosy mist still holding late marvellous
Sun-glow, the air smelt home; the time breathed home.
Noel not put away; new term not yet come,
All things said 'Severn', the air was of those calm meadows;
Transport rattled somewhere in the southern shadows;
Stars that were not strange ruled the most quiet high
Arch of soft sky, starred and most grave to see, most high.
What should break that but gun-noise or last Trump?
But neither came. At sudden, with light jump
Clarinet sang into 'Hundred Pipers and A'',
Aveluy's Scottish answered with pipers' true call
'Happy we've been a' tegether'. When nothing
Stayed of war-weariness or Winter's loathing,
Crackers with Christmas stockings hung in the heavens,
Gladness split discipline in sixes and sevens,
Hunger ebb'd magically mixed with strange leavens;
Forgotten, forgotten the hard time's true clothing,
And stars were happy to see Man making Fate plaything.

The Abbey

If I could know the quarry where these stones grew
A thousand years ago; I would turn east now
And climb Portway with my blood fretted all grew
With the frightened beeches with that strange wind-kindled rough
    row.

And there, grown over with blackberry and perhaps stray ferns
Willowherb, tansy, horehound, other wonders (here to come)
I should find a wide pit fit for a masque (if the turns
Of such should ever again) with tree screens and robing room.

I Saw England (July Night)

She was a village
Of lovely knowledge
The high roads left her aside, she was forlorn, a maid —
Water ran there, dusk hid her, she climbed four-wayed.
Brown-gold windows showed last folk not yet asleep;
Water ran, was a centre of silence deep,
Fathomless deeps of pricked sky, almost fathomless
Hallowed an upward gaze in pale satin of blue.
And I was happy indeed, of mind, soul, body even
Having got given
A sign undoubtful of a dear England few
Doubt, not many have seen,
That Will Squele he knew and so was shriven.
Home of Twelfth Night — Edward Thomas by Arras fallen,
Borrow and Hardy, Sussex tales out of Roman heights callen.
No madrigals or field-songs to my all reverent whim;
Till I got back I was dumb.

First Time In

The Captain addressed us. After glow grew deeper,
Like England, like the West Country, and stars grew thicker.
In silence we left the billet, we found the hard roadway
In single file, jangling (silent) and on the gray
Chipped road, moaned over ever by snipers' shots.
Got shelter in the first trench; and the thud of boots
On duckboard wood from grate on rough road stone it changed.
(Verey lights showed ghastly, and a machine gun ranged.)
Sentry here and there. How the trench wound now! Wires
Hindered, thistles pricked, but few guns spat their fires.
Upward a little . . . wider a little, the Reserve Line reached.
Tin hat shapes, dark body shapes and faces as bleached.
And the heart's beat: 'Here men are maimed and shot through, hit
     through;
Here iron and lead rain, sandbags rent in two,
And the honours are earned. The stuff of tales is woven.'
Here were whispers of encouragement, above the cloven
Trenches faces showed and West soft somethings were said,
Lucky were signallers who (intellectual) strangely had
Some local independence in Line danger, but
In training or on Rest were from honour shut.
Bundling over sky lines to clear trench digging —
On the Plain scorn went with tapping and flag wagging
Directions. And then one took us courteously
Where a sheet lifted, and gold light cautiously
Streamed from an oilsheet slitted vertical into
Half light of May. We entered, took stranger-view
Of life as lived in the Line, the Line of war and daily
Papers, dispatches, brave-soldier talks, the really, really
Truly Line; and these the heroes of story.

Never were quieter folk in teaparty history.
Never in *Cranford*, Trollope, even. And as it were, home
Closed round us. They told us lore, how and when did come

Minnie-werfers and grenades from over there east;
The pleasant and unpleasant habits of the beast
That crafted and tore Europe. What Line mending was
When guns centred and dugouts rocked in a haze
And hearing was — (wires cut) — All necessary
Common sense workmanlike cautions of salutary
Wisdom — the mechanic day-lore of modern war-making,
Calm thought discovered in mind and body-shaking.
The whole craft and business of bad occasion.
Talk turned personal, and to borders of two nations
Gone out; Cotswold's Black Mountain edges against august
August after-sun's glow, and air a lit dust
With motes and streams of gold. Wales Her soul visible
Against all power West Heaven ever could flood full.
And of songs — the 'Slumber Song', and the soft Chant
So beautiful to which Rabelaisian songs were meant;
Of South and North Wales; and 'David of the White Rock':
What an evening! What a first time, what a shock
So rare of home-pleasure beyond measure
And always to Time's ending surely a treasure,
After-War so surely hurt, disappointed men
Who looked for the Golden Age to come friendly again.
With inn evenings of meetings in warm glows,
Talk: coal and wood fire uttering rosy shows
With beer and 'Widdicombe Fair' and five mile homeward —
Moonlight lying thick on frost spangled fleet foot sward,
And owl crying out every short while his one evil word.

At any rate, disputeless the romantic evening was —
The night, the midnight; next day Fritz strafed at us,
And I lay belly upward to wonder: when — but useless.

The Unvisited Church

Disappointment comes to all men, if so the church
So long looked at and left aside proved faultful, then
It were better to reflect — Had I followed the urge
And visited that, by reason of a Norman arch
Not there, but reasonably looked for, then the reproach
I had not felt, to have feared leaving the high road,
To have ridden on, busy, or too careless to approach
And the thought left hidden to rankle and goad —
But now the thing is seen and the regret taken:
The hill known nobler than the guarding tower;
A resolve has been acted on, and a faith shaken
That Severn churches all were of England, Her flower.
Romance would have remained had I had less courage —
But truth came to me in my trouble of hour —
To decide whether or not — I should venture the search;
Or ride on to my tested and well-loved things.
But it was better to look and be disappointed
Than not to look, — it was adventure, and though the so-wanted
Beauty was not found truth was kept, and comes out of ruth.

Brimscombe

One lucky hour in middle of my tiredness
I came under the pines of the sheer steep
And saw the stars like steady candles gleam
Above and through them; Brimscombe wrapped past life in sleep!
Such body weariness and ugliness
Had gone before, such tiredness to come on me
This perfect moment had such pure clemency
That it my memory has all coloured since,

Forgetting the blackness and pain so driven hence,
And the naked uplands from even bramble free,
That ringed-in hour of pines, stars and dark eminence;
(The thing we looked for in our fear of France.)

Poem For End

So the last poem is laid flat in its place,
And Crickley with Crucifix Corner leaves from my face
Elizabethans and night-working thoughts — of such grace.

And all the dawns that set my thoughts new to making;
Or Crickley dusk that the beech leaves stirred to shaking
Are put aside — there is a book ended; heart aching.

Joy and sorrow, and all thoughts a poet thinks,
Walking or turning to music; the wrought out links
Of fancy to fancy — by Severn or by Artois brinks.

Only what's false in this, blood itself would not save,
Sweat would not heighten — the dead Master in his grave
Would my true following of him, my care approve.

And more than he, I paid the prices of life
Standing where Rome immortal heard October's strife,
A war poet whose right of honour cuts falsehood like a knife.

War poet — his right is of nobler steel — the careful sword —
And night walker will not suffer of praise the word
From the sleepers; the custom-followers, the dead lives unstirred.

Only, who thought of England as two thousand years
Must keep of today's life, the proper anger and fears,
England that was paid for by building and ploughing and tears.

Textual Notes

These notes offer an abbreviated account of the lengthy and some-
times convoluted textual history of *Rewards of Wonder*. For reasons of
brevity and clarity, only those manuscripts, typescripts and printed
texts which have a direct bearing on that history have been included
here. So, for example, no reference has been made to the masses of
typescripts produced by Gurney's friends and supporters in their
attempts to preserve and popularise his work, except where those
typescripts represent the only surviving evidence of a particular stage
in the development of the collection. Similarly, the inclusion of indi-
vidual poems from *Rewards of Wonder* in posthumous editions of
Gurney's work has been noted but no other information about these
particular texts has been given.

The notes themselves use certain typographic devices to describe
the origins, development and publication history of each poem:

•	a bullet-point indicates that this particular version of a poem is previously unpublished.
GMS64.3.41v	manuscripts or typescripts are listed using a two-part citation system: the letters indicate the *original* status of the material, the abbreviations used for this purpose being listed in chronological order on pages 104 to 107, whilst the numbers give its *present* location in the Gurney Archive. This is necessary because some groups of material have, in the past, been broken up and re-ordered several times, meaning that a single location in the Gurney Archive can now contain texts from up to a dozen different sources.
1RVW16.9	bold type indicates the manuscript or typescript which has been used as copy-text for this edition.
1982.140	italic type indicates a published text, with the page number being given after the full stop.
1954.85	bold and italic type indicates the published text

	which has been used as copy-text for this edition.
~~of mortar shot~~	strikethrough indicates a word or phrase deleted in the original manuscript.
{deep}	angled brackets indicate a word or phrase written above or below the line and marked with an arrow to show where it should be inserted into the text.
Rome	arial type indicates the revisions that Gurney made to the green hardback manuscript notebook in February 1925.

The numerous textual variants referred to in the notes are indicated by the following sigla:

Manuscripts and Typescripts in the Gurney Archive

LS   Eight 257mm × 210mm feint-ruled loose sheets, containing three fair-copy poems written in black ink. Undated but probably produced in the second half of 1921.

EB   Nine 214mm × 170mm feint-ruled pages torn from a missing exercise book, containing nine poems written in blue ink. Undated, but handwriting and textual evidence suggest the mid to late 1921 period. Used by Dorothy Gurney in 1922 to create the typescripts for her brother's rejected third book (Walter & Thornton 1997: 6–7, 9–10).

BMS   210mm × 162mm black hard-cover feint-ruled exercise book. Seventy-one pages with one page torn out. A hundred and two poems, many fragmentary and unfinished, written in black ink in a clean, neat hand. The inside front cover reads: 'I B Gurney | 1 Westfield Terrace | Longford | Gloucester'. The inside back cover reads: 'the act of writing is a distraction in madness'. Undated, but the handwriting and address suggest the late 1921 to late 1922 period.

GMS   214mm × 170mm green hard-cover feint-ruled exercise book. Sixty-three pages plus two 235mm × 180mm loose wide feint-ruled sheets inserted at back. Pages obviously torn out. Seventy-nine poems, many incomplete, written untidily in grey-blue ink. Frequent crossings-out, with later corrections and additions in black or very dark blue ink. The title page reads: 'the Note book | (between music | makings) | of Ivor Gurney | 1921–1922 | corrected. | Feb 1925. | Ivor Gurney.'

PMS   237mm × 182mm pink marbled effect hard-cover feint-ruled exercise book. Ninety-five pages with two torn out. One hundred and thirty eight poems, some fragmentary and unfinished. The majority of texts are written in black ink, with some in pencil; all are untidy in appearance, with various crossings-out and obvious signs of drafting. The inside front cover reads: 'Music to Miss C Rogers | Music Publisher | Berners St London W | Poetry to Professor Saintsbury | Bath'. Written in a very disturbed hand on the inside back cover is: 'instead of a home | I require death'. In use between early 1922 and late 1922.

GTS   Five 257mm × 205mm vertical line wiremarked pages containing four poems from GMS typed in double-line spacing with titles in capitals underlined with double solid red lines. The title page reads: 'THIRD VOLUME OF POEMS | BY | IVOR GURNEY | THE GREEN MANUSCRIPT BOOK'. Either typed by Marion Scott or produced at her instigation between late 1922 and early 1923.

PTS   Ninety-two 626mm × 213mm horizontal line wiremarked pages, containing eighty-six poems from PMS typed using double-line spacing with titles in capitals and underlined with either double solid red lines or a solid red line above a broken red line. The majority are carbon copies corrected by Ivor Gurney in blue ink. Many poems have typed textual footnote initialled 'M.M.S.', suggesting that they were typed either by Marion Scott or at her instigation between late 1922 and early 1923.

MMS   Nineteen 230mm × 327mm vertical wiremarked sheets, containing thirty-nine poems in Marion Scott's handwriting, written in blue-black ink. The first sheet is headed 'Gurney's Poems'. Undated, but annotations in ink and pencil giving directions to typist suggest that these manuscripts were produced in 1928 for the proposed Gollancz edition of Gurney's poems.

1RVW   Eighty-three 264mm × 213 mm 'Royal Charter Bond' water-marked containing eighty-one poems taken from the missing Mollie Hart typescript of *Rewards of Wonder*, typed using single line spacing. All pages are numbered; titles are given in capitals and underlined with a single solid line, with a single solid line at the end of each text. The title page reads: 'REWARDS OF WONDER. | [rule 83mm] | Poems of Cotswold, France, London. | --- by --- | IVOR Gurney | [rule 54mm]'. A manuscript note above this in pencil by Edmund Blunden dated '18 v 51' lists seventeen poems removed for 'the Selection'. Typed by 'a very good typist in Dorking' in 1943 at the instigation of Ralph Vaughan Williams.

Periodicals and Anthologies Published During Gurney's Lifetime
1924a   *The London Mercury*, Volume IX, Number 51 (January 1924)
1924b   *Second Selections From Modern Poets*, made by J. C. Squire (London: Martin Secker, 1924)
1927   *Music and Letters*, Volume VIII, Number 2 (April 1927)
1931   *The Mercury Book of Verse*, with an introduction by Sir Henry Newbolt (London: Macmillan and Co., 1931)
1932   *Younger Poets of Today*, selected by J. C. Squire (London: Martin Secker, 1932)
1933   *The London Mercury*, Volume XXIX, Number 170 (December 1933)
1934a   *The London Mercury*, Volume XXIX, Number 171 (January 1934)
1934b   *The London Mercury*, Volume XXX, Number 178 (August 1934)

Posthumous Editions of Gurney's Poems
1954   *Poems by Ivor Gurney*, edited with a memoir by Edmund Blunden (London: Hutchinson, 1954)

1973   *Poems of Ivor Gurney 1890–1937*, edited by Leonard Clark
          (London: Chatto & Windus, 1973)
1982   *Collected Poems of Ivor Gurney*, chosen and edited by P. J.
          Kavanagh (London: Oxford University Press, 1982)
1996   *Ivor Gurney: Selected Poems*, edited with an introduction by
          George Walter (London: Everyman's Poetry Library, 1996)
1997   *Ivor Gurney: 80 Poems or So*, edited by George Walter & R.
          K. R. Thornton (Ashington & Manchester: MidNAG &
          Carcanet, 1997)

Rewards of Wonder: Poems of Cotswold, France, London

p.23   *The Lantern-Shine.* • GMS64.3.3, **1RVW16.7**. Lines 11 to 13 in GMS
          read:
          > Where fear was, once gloriously {walked through and all} fought
          > ~~Going since night was doubtfully night~~
          > Doubtfully proceeding past Autumn-crocus meadow,
          > And the camp where Rome made dark triumph high over Autumn
          > night.

p.23   *October.* • GMS64.3.53, **1RVW16.8**. GMS ends on line 17, with line 4
          reading: 'Realty in ~~the~~ Gehenna a sick mind roams.'

p.24   *Glory — and Quiet Glory.* • GMS64.3.41v, **1RVW16.9**. GMS is called
          'The Spirit of Man' and ends on line 14.

p.25   *Half Dead.* PMS64.1.6, PTS16.13, **MMS64.11.124**, 1RVW16.11,
          1973.71, *1982.81–82*, *1996.32*. PMS and PTS lack lines 9 and 11 and
          end on the phrase 'seeing rare' in line 12.

p.26   *Tobacco.* PMS64.1.4–5, **MMS64.11.129–129v**, *1954.72–73*, *1973.60–
          61*, *1982.61–63*, *230–231*, *1996.31–32*. PMS lacks lines 9, 45 and 46 and
          ends on line 58, but includes a false start for line 54: '~~The hunger for
          Empire vegetable diet | Taken into the lungs soaked deep and quiet~~'.

p.28   *Laventie Dawn.* • GMS64.3.7, *1924a.236*, *1924b.222*, **1RVW16.14**,
          1973.58–59. GMS lacks a title and, in place of lines 8 to 16, has:
          > First light bringing the thought what familiar star
          > There was of town, farm, cottage, over yonder . . . .
          > And all an exile's longing for the dear
          > Sight of great Severn plain by mist wraiths whitened.

          1924a prints the text as a continuation of 'Smudgy Dawn', replacing
          lines 8 to 16 with:
          > First light bringing the thought what familiar star
          > There was, of town, farm, cottage, over there, over yonder,
          > And by day before duty settled awhile to

A companionship of good talk, forgetting night's woe.

1924b, however, restores 'Laventie Dawn' to its original status as a separate poem and prints it with the conjectural title 'Dawn'.

p.28   *Leckhampton Elbow.* • GMS64.3.8, **1RVW16.15**. GMS is called 'Leckhampton' and reads:

> Wraith of grey cloud in Leckhampton elbow —
> A queer unlooked for relic of short storm
> Impelled by air unfelt by the walker below;
> Gave thought how I had left by Crickley a kite
> To hover in such a mist above the Rome-height
> And grassed slopes of the very old, and soldier bold
> Camp of the deserted routine of old soldier-hold.
> A thing of eternal interest, the kite hovering
> Below the beech clump above small firs covering
> A spinnies breadth with green colour and light sighs ——
> And the white farm there I had worked from and got wages;
> But here was Leckhampton, and 5 miles to go . . . .
> The Devil's Chimney to watch for its queerness of ages
> (That since has collapsed — to the Devil's regret melancholy woe)
> And to remember poetry from other men's pages,
> To see the linnets and light starlings go.

p.29   *Tobacco.* GMS64.3.62–62v, *1924a.236–237*, *1931.130–131*, *1932.220–221*. GMS is titleless and lacks lines 13 to 14 and 29 to 30. The curious italicisation of lines 29, 30 and 33 in *1924a* is not repeated in *1931* and *1932*, suggesting a momentary whim on J. C. Squire's part. However, it is not unknown for Gurney to underline words and phrases in his manuscripts and there is no obvious reason for Squire to italicise these lines unless he was following instructions on his copy-text.

p.30   *Queen of Cotswold.* • GMS64.3.5, **1RVW16.16**. In place of lines 9 to 24, GMS has:

> ~~And~~ Heavy on hope ~~aloud~~ not blind to ~~most~~ inevitable ~~certain~~ gray —
> ~~And~~ Gray soothed and smoothed ~~by~~ out by beauty, by grave beauty
> Although no weather wonder can hide the poverty, sorrow under.

p.31   *By Severn.* GMS64.3.25, *1954.75*, *1982.145–146*, *1996.52*. GMS lacks line 14 but includes an additional last line: 'As dear Chaucer prayed.'

p.32   *The Tax Office.* • GMS64.3.25v & 27v, **1RVW16.17**. GMS includes a false start for line 35 – '~~Steep the guarding pastures of pop~~' – and ends on line 39.

p.33   *Praise of Tobacco.* • GMS64.3.9, **1RVW16.18**. GMS lacks line 3 and, in place of lines 6 to 19, has:

> To say an admiration of what may soothe
> The bitterest (nearly) of unearned ruth —

And join~~ed~~ the happiest calm-tune with its grace.
(Curling in loveliest fashion of line and wreath)
Who reads "Collected works" may find much, in short space,
Of praise, and wit, and most masculine blunt rebuke,
But here's writ only the frame of a praise of a truth
Known to a world's end — the worth, delight of tobacco ——
Without that great manner to give the verse honour.
But if the reader dislike he may turn his back so
As to insult one who will take revenge (if he manage)
By reading the Epigrams with a pipe all full in glow.

p.34   *Laventie.* PMS64.1.7–8, **MMS64.11.132–132v**, *1954.69–70*, *1982.*
       77–78, *1996.53–54*. PMS lacks lines 14 and 22 to 23 and ends on line
       44.

p.35   *April is Happy.* • GMS64.3.27, **1RVW16.19**.

p.36   *The Ford.* • GMS64.3.31v, **MMS64.11.128**, 1RVW16.20. GMS lacks
       line 17.

p.36   *The Bargain.* • GMS64.3.7v, **1RVW16.21**. In place of lines 9 to 19,
       GMS has: 'The Navy of Spain riding equal the Atlantic Main, | Dissolved
       like fog shapes or the mist of drouth.'

p.37   *Darkness Has Cheating Swiftness.* • GMS64.3.4, *1933.103*, **1RVW16.22.1**,
       1973.82–83, *1982.81*, *1996.30*. Lines 11 and 12 in GMS and *1933* read:
       'Long stretched out in bright sparkles of gratefullest | Homecalling
       array.'

p.38   *Student Days.* • GMS64.3.33v, **1RVW16.23**. GMS is called 'Alter-
       nations' and, in place of lines 5 to 12, has:
       Nor is the princely or most maidenly beauty
       Of Crickley or Cranham known whether on their own roads
       Or from the valley looking friendly to old majesty.
       The day clouds or the mind clouds, there is never the time
       Happy-all for music or the fashioning of rhyme.

p.38   *The Ford.* • GMS64.3.34v, **MMS64.11.124v**, 1RVW16.24. The final
       stanza in GMS reads:
       A dead thing panged with life, or a life ~~racked or~~ {and} hung heavy
       With death? No matter. There was business to do away back there
       And a {Inn} coat of arms marked with the dangerous wavy
       Signs, half a day to go, and new hands at the rack here

p.39   *The Touchstone (Watching Malvern).* GMS64.3.61v, *1954.83*, *1973.126*,
       1982.79. This form of the title is taken from the index to the first version
       of *Rewards of Wonder*.

p.39   *Thoughts of New England.* GMS64.3.36–36v,64,37–38,65, LS64.12.
       34–37, *1924a.232–234*, *1924b.215–220*, *1996.46–49*. GMS is clearly a
       first draft and contains a number of false starts, such as '~~Wondering~~
       ~~what new land felt like to wit~~' for line 15 and '~~And curfew rings in lanes~~

~~half light at even~~' for line 25. However, it also shows extensive signs of
later revisions, which seem to have been done in the summer of 1924
and not in February 1925 as elsewhere in the notebook: an appeal to
John Haines *circa* July 1924 talks of 'the longer version of the New
England poem — three times rewritten — twice as long — twice as
good', echoing a note at the bottom of page 65 of GMS, which reads:
'3rd version — better than first. less than second'. In order to create this
'3rd version', Gurney has inserted new lines wherever he can find a
space in the manuscript: 'Matching their strength to such noble places,
and History's ways.' appears between lines 48 and 49, whilst '(The
careful outcome of wide Europe's treasure.)' comes between lines 51
and 52; '(And the longing of this one valley is like hunger.)' is inserted
between lines 72 and 73, and '(The new lands have not the old beauty
yet outwrested.)' is placed where line 77 appears in the printed text.
Similarly, the last stanza of the poem has been torn out and replaced
with two pages of new material, with these and the remaining sections of
the original draft being numbered to show where this new material
should be inserted. Section 3 comes between lines 31 and 32:

> Yes, of Massachussetts they think and the old drum
> which turned their forbears to see the new lands, and strive
> Hardly or easily with ploughlands of new names . . . .
> musing awhile of old names of chronicled high fames
> And of the bitterness which moved them to seek a life
> Far from the Leadon's quietness or the birth of Thames
>
> They watched the Massachussetts land, and thanked God to come
> Into a free land, might be their all-loved home,
> Save for the newness of all things, and never the flames
> Of old story suddenly bursting out from the deep loam,
> (or clay) and thought how worship here might have it's course . . . .
> But where was Gloucester tower standing above the alive
> Valley of spring, and where was Tewkesbury to be known?
> (Crying rough rebukes to the straining uncomprehending horse)
> Thanking so much, after the waste of dangerous-pass foam —
> Regretting so much the age hallowed beauty, and the sha
> or triumphs of battle, that to the older earth continual cleave?

and section 7 comes after line 81:

> Or high clouds in array by sunsets wind ranged.
> Better to stay, and remember the old names of the earls
> Who gave the Crecy window, after unnamed valours,
> To be the wonder of April for half morning colours.
> Or the builders of small churches or of Deerhurst's might,
> Or Corse's beauty by Staunton from heart estranged.

The New World has qualities, Her great own,
But the Old not yet decrepit or worn is grown,
And brick and timber of age five centuries known
Are consolations for bare poverty enough
Against New York, where they say Opera is brilliant
And the bye-ways with five-dollar notes are strown.
(For all the glory of Whitman in his words surge and plan)
the stuff of Liberty is a varying stuff,
And the nobleness of the Civil war being had aware;
My County requires longer and more coloured proof;
Yet from the armies of conflict that fought, and grew gaunt —
(the Armies of the Carolinas or Illinois alone enough)
From Grant's men, or Lee's men nobleness should never want.

LS is a fair copy of the uncorrected GMS text and only differs from
1924a in ending on line 88.

In an asylum letter to Marion Scott written in November 1924,
Gurney complains bitterly about 'damned misprints alterations' in the
1924b text of 'Thoughts of New England'. These are mostly minor —
'wandering' for 'wondering' in line 9, for example, or a missing hyphen
in 'asphalt-paved' in line 45 — but another letter written at the same
time to Annie Nelson Drummond talks of two substantive 'damned
mistakes' and lists them: 'town. for World' and 'noblemen for noble-
ness'. These errors occur in lines 52 and 89 of *1924b* and, because
Squire's copy-text is now no longer extant, they cannot be checked.
However, in all other asylum texts of the poem where they appear, the
corrected forms of these lines are used, which suggests that Gurney had
a genuine grievance. They have accordingly been amended here, and the
'new' that precedes 'World' has been capitalised for the sake of agree-
ment. A further correction to line 89 mentioned in this letter — 'Grants
men Lees men | for centuries Chivalrous order' — does not appear in
any manuscript of the poem, suggesting a momentary whim on
Gurney's part, and so has been ignored.

At the same time, Gurney also produced a series of rewritings of all
of the poems that appeared in Squire's anthology — four new texts of
'Thoughts of New England', six pages of 'Additions' for the same poem
and new versions of the two other texts that Squire had printed,
'Smudgy Dawn' and 'Dawn' — but they are so radically different from
their original sources that they have not been included here.

p.42   *When The Sun Leaps Tremendous.* • GMS64.3.26v, **MMS64.11.134**,
1RVW16.27. GMS is called 'Sunrising' and, in place of lines 4 to 15,
has:

    And the land breathes of the happiness of his love or his powers

All the day the townsfolk shall live {as} in a day space. dim,
For recognitions, while the country shall move in, breathe the airs
Tiniest he has quickened, friendly with birds and flowers ——
(Taking his down swerving but as Majesty's whim)
Till the stars end their routine — and peace comforts their cares.

p.43 *Canadians.* PMS64.1.15, PTS16.30, **1RVW16.29**, *1973.66, 1982.87,*
      1996.54–55. Both PMS and PTS lack line 11, have an alternative line 16
      — 'Saskatchewan, Ontario, Jack London ran in' — and end on line 20.

p.44 *Severn Meadows.* • PMS64.1.19v, PTS16.32, **1RVW16.31.** PMS and
      PTS both end on line 8.

p.44 *After War — Half War.* PMS64.1.21, PTS16.34, **1RVW16.33,** *1973.87,*
      1982.84. This poem is called 'After War' in PMS and PTS and both lack
      lines 7, 10 and 11.

p.45 *The Ford.* • PMS64.1.9, **MMS64.11.128v.** PMS ends on the word
      'gaping' in line 7.

p.45 *Laventie Front.* • GMS64.3.9v & 12v, **MMS64.11.131–131v,**
      1RVW16.37. GMS lacks lines 10, 17 and 27 to 29 and, in place of lines
      40 and 41 has: 'Upward and upward till full day was proved and loved
      — | And the minnie werfers began their deadly worryings.'

p.47 *Cyril Tourneur.* • PMS64.1.22, **1RVW16.41.** PMS ends on line 12. Page
      65 of PMS contains another version of this poem, 'Master Cyril
      Tourneur', which was also revised and included in *Poems by Ivor
      Gurney (The Marbled Book, with later Additions).*

p.47 *Of Cruelty.* GMS64.3.30v, *1954.77, 1982.195–196, 1996.55.* GMS has
      been retitled 'Of ~~Cruelty~~ {Garden stuff}' and, in place of line 4, has:
      'grub holed it is ~~drained~~ {drawn} upward, from the earth scarred.' It
      ends on line 14, which reads: 'And anxieties ~~and mixed~~ of mind for the
      penny or two will a base meal win.'

p.48 *First March.* PMS64.1.16, **1RVW16.44,** *1982.75–76* 3. PMS lacks lines
      3 and 22 and ends on line 23, with line 17 reading: 'being ~~the one way
      not to die~~ {the one thought under by.}'

p.49 *Of Bricks and Brick Pits.* • PMS64.1.17, PTS16.46, **1RVW16.45.** PMS
      and PTS are both titleless and lack lines 14 and 18, ending on the word
      'fill' in line 17. The index to the first version of *Rewards of Wonder* lists
      a poem called 'Of Birds' in place of this one, a title which bears no rela-
      tion to any poem amongst either the *Rewards of Wonder* material or their
      variants. Given that PTS bears no title and that any title added during
      corrections would thus be in Gurney's often obscure handwriting, it
      seems most likely that 'Of Birds' is Mollie Hart's misreading of the
      phrase 'Of Bricks'.

p.50 *Cotswold Slopes.* • GMS64.3.21–21v, **1RVW16.47.** In place of lines 15 to
      19, GMS has: 'Cotswold shows all that county extending {far} battle-
      ment, | And the strict fall of Crickley's {loved} masterful~~princee~~lness —'

and, in place of lines 30 to 32, has:

> Thinks of the walker he sees, both are lonely talker
> With the wondered at trees, clouds, colours of the thousand foot
> High plain —— And of the Mother there is never a doubt
> (Earth the Mother) who calls the soul still as strong
> As if the Briton, hHer dear Child moved among ——
> Or if Roman was the speech of his enrapturing tongue.

p.51 *Robecq.* • PMS64.1.19, PTS16.49, 1RVW16.48. PMS and PTS both end on line 5.

p.51 *Near Vermand.* PMS64.1.25, PTS16.52, 1RVW16.51, *1973.69, 1982.83, 1996.33.* PMS and PTS both end on the word 'digging' in line 10.

p.52 *The Cloud.* GMS64.3.22–22v, *1924a.235, 1954.78, 1973.59, 1982.128, 1996.56.* GMS lacks lines 13 and 14.

p.52 *At the Inn.* • GMS64.3.35, 1RVW16.53. In place of lines 5 to 12, GMS has:

> "I'm Twe Seventeen Come Sunday" —— their fathers had sung . . . .
> "Golden Vanity" they once knew when the world was more
>   young . . . .
> But my cold and my love of the land, forbade all
> My scorn of my hate for the town-stuff of music-hall.
>
> I rested and listened to words of Shallow and Will Squele.

p.53 *Of Trees Over There.* • PMS64.1.16v, 1RVW16.54. In place of lines 2 and 3, PMS has 'Or decayed teeth, or mere unsightly lumps, | And plane trees most useful saving borders' and lacks lines 6, 16 and 25. The correct spelling of 'La Gorgues' in line 9 is in fact 'La Gorgue', a spelling also used in 'Gifts and Courtesy', but uses both forms in the PMS text of 'La Gorgues'. This suggests that Gurney regarded either as acceptable and, accordingly, no amendment has been made here.

p.54 *Gifts and Courtesy.* • GMS64.3.38v, 1RVW16.55. This poem is called 'Horror has died now' in GMS and the index to the first version of *Rewards of Wonder*; GMS has been retitled '{Change in Memory}' and, in place of lines 4 to 23, has:

> Of fatigue, But there was one gift
> café-au-lait by La Gorgues where the river goes . . . .
> A kindness near Vaux, a sight of snowdrops in a left-
> by-Chance garden of the German Retreat, that falls
> As sweetly now to the memory as almost then to me
> Then It did, for strangeness of courtesy and generosity.
> (And the wonder of finding unbroken gracious Nesles,)
> So the memory hides up what never could have
> Happened — the triple-agonies, and all-denials,

To a sort of Romance of foreign and unashamed soldiery.

p.55 *Roman, and the War Poet.* • GMS64.3.39, 1RVW16.56. This poem is
called 'White Slopes' in both GMS and the index to the first version of
Rewards of Wonder. GMS, in place of lines 9 to 16, has:

But I cried "Romans, I also have passed

Ages of night watching in a Roman place

Got wound, against foe, in the drear night (blood cold, frozen iced)

And sang songs of battle, and had danger's pride ~~and~~ in war's days."

p.55 *Kilns.* GMS64.3.40–40v, *1954.76*, *1982.126–127*, *1996.56–57*. '(the
Danes new conquerors from the North Seas fiercely in-wayed.)' is
inserted between lines 19 and 20 in GMS, which also has two additional
last lines: 'The reeves or the craftsmen coming with suddenness, save |
Some neighbour warned them, the King's men were after worrying
them.'

p.57 *Riez Bailleul.* PMS64.1.22v, PTS16.58, 1RVW16.57, *1973.70*,
1982.84–85. The manuscripts of 'Riez Bailleul' and 'Riez Bailleul Also'
appear on facing pages in PMS and, given the latter's lack of a title, it is
evident that they were originally all one poem. This arrangement is
followed in the index to the first version of *Rewards of Wonder*, where
'Riez Bailleul Also' is absent and 'Rivy Bailleul' — typists frequently
misread Gurney's lower case 'z' as 'y' — is listed as occupying pages 51
and 52. When Gurney came to revise the collection, he added a new fifth
stanza to 'Riez Bailleul' and added lines 6 to 10 to the original fifth
stanza to create 'Riez Bailleul Also'.

p.58 *Riez Bailleul Also.* • PMS64.1.23, 1RVW16.59, *1982.85*.

p.58 *What I Will Pay.* GMS64.3.56v, 1RVW16.60, *1982.76*. This is another
poem missing from the index to the first version of *Rewards of Wonder*.
The version in GMS is called 'Prices' and reads:

What I will pay to my God is that I will not sleep between ~~the~~ cool
sheets

Neither encourage tiredness in limbs ~~that were~~ as desirous after
heights as the bird that fleets

Scorning intellect ~~as~~, loving the middle path, living without envy and
~~in~~ but worthy fear.

But now without pause or tiredness the day must move to a dull
routine end here

In mists of doubt of worthiness, never to God or man the purposing
clear . . . . .

Never the clear spirit sure of it's truth — but always at doubts and
debates.

p.59 *Smudgy Dawn.* EB70.34, GMS64.3.10, *1924a.236*, *1924b.221*,
MMS64.11.136v, *1954.84*, *1973.58*, *1982.143*, *1996.49–50*, *1997.46*.
This poem is called 'Spring Dawn' in EB and ends on line 10, whilst

GMS has '(O Gloucester, County of Beauty, honour of man and the All-Maker.)' in place of lines 11 to 12. *1924a* lacks lines 11 to 12 and instead prints 'Laventie Dawn' as a second stanza.

p.60   *Crucifix Corner.* PMS64.1.10–10v, **MMS64.11.136**, *1954.68*, *1982.80–81*. PMS lacks line 22 and ends on line 26 with the words 'time's true clothing'.

p.61   *Half Dead.* • GMS64.3.10v, **1RVW16.61**. GMS includes an additional final line: '(The March stars in their course majestic inwoven.)'

p.61   *Today.* • PMS64.1.24, PTS16.63, **1RVW16.62**. PMS and PTS both end on line 8.

p.62   *Early Spring Dawn.* PMS64.1.26, *1934a.204*, **1954.79**, *1973.125–126*, *1982.129*.

p.62   *First Time In.* PMS64.1.27, **MMS64.11.135**, 1RVW16.64, *1982.69*, *1996*.58. PMS lacks line 13 and ends on line 14.

p.63   *Cotswold.* • PMS64.1.28v, PTS16.66, **1RVW16.65**. PMS and PTS both end on line 6.

p.63   *The Song.* • GMS64.3.11v-12, **1RVW16.67**. GMS lacks line 11 and ends on line 22.

p.64   *La Gorgues.* PMS64.1.11–11v, **1RVW16.68**, *1982.69–70*, *1996.58–59*. PMS ends on line 28.

p.65   *Northleach.* • GMS64.3.12, **1RVW16.69**. GMS contains only the first two and a half lines of this poem, heavily deleted.

p.66   *Clouds Die Out In June.* GMS64.3.13, **1RVW16.70**, *1982.70*. GMS is called 'June Night' and, in place of lines 4 to 20, has:

> Stars as bright sand grains remain, and the skies high dun sacred glow.
> Out of the earth comes sacredness for the blood,
> From the rapt heavens comes majesty to the mood;
> Being is caught inspired as the poet is fired;
> And till the dawn light no heart's longing ever is tired.

p.67   *Blighty.* GMS64.3.32, **1RVW16.71**, *1982.71*, *1996.59–60*. This poem is called 'The Landing' in GMS and line 19 reads: '~~Matron of workhouses, not mistress of the sea.~~ {Southampton, name of tales of many landings from the World's Sea}'.

p.67   *The Bargain.* GMS64.3.14–14v, **1RVW16.73**, *1982.71–72*. GMS ends on the phrase 'a {Council} rubbish heap.' in line 25.

p.68   *Laventie Ridge.* • PMS64.1.29, **1RVW16.74**. PMS lacks the third and fourth stanzas.

p.69   *Sheer Falls of Green Slope.* • GMS64.3.15, **1RVW16.75**. This poem is called 'Slopes known of old' in GMS and lacks lines 6, 16 and 17.

p.70   *The Essential Things.* • GMS64.3.16v, **1RVW16.76**.

p.70   *If Ben Jonson Were Back.* • GMS64.3.20v, **1RVW16.77**. GMS lacks line 10 and, in place of lines 12 to 20, has:

The shopmen, knaves, gulls, queer characters of all London town.
But, after correcting his Commemoratory verses
(And seeing of his last or favourite plays the rehearses)
He took a brave farewell of what he loved all well.
Strand, Aldgate, Alsatia, and Whitechapel —
And having praised his Master as Time outlaster,
Went out into another life with a great "<u>Farewell</u>".

p.71   *Tewkesbury*. • GMS64.3.23, **1RVW16.78**. In place of lines 15 and 16, GMS has:

Shall so run when villas ~~stand where~~ cover the defiled land.
(But may some kind Hell clean her of that defile!)
Tewkesbury, loved of long Centuries honour as grand
The Valley while Severn meets Avon and marries one.

p.72   *Old Tale*. EB64.12.6, GMS64.3.24, *1924a.235*, **MMS64.11.136v**, 1RVW16.79, *1973.62, 1982.82, 1996.29–30, 1997.125*. This poem is called 'Daily' in EB and has 'so lumbering and slow' in place of 'I'll sheathe my own' in line 7, a reading followed by *1924a*.

p.72   *Thoughts on Beethoven*. • GMS64.3.51v, **1RVW16.80**, *1927.103, 1954.94, 1973.67–68, 1982.77, 1996.71*. GMS reads:

Beethoven I wronged thee undernoting thus
Thy dignity and worth; the overplus
Of one quartett almost would our book overweigh —
Almost chosen out at random from your own day
You have our great Ben's mastery and a freer
Carriage of method, spice of the open air . . . . .
Which he our greatest builder had not so:
Not as his own at least, but acquiréd-to.
~~They this~~ {(May)} no false fashion put thy {true} fame away
As in Vienna, when wantons ~~first~~ {laid all} away
Thy ~~s~~work Homeric for a {soft} Southern zephyr —
And ~~that~~ heroes were no other than as {day's} heifer
Sacrificed on the altar of worlds praise;
The amusement or brittle heightening of drab days.

Whereas thy sinewed strength is by Aeschylus
Homer, Ben Jonson, Shakespeare and a pillar of us.
Master. Such are our memories which ~~false~~ do never betray
~~The thought of daylight even in the minds gray~~
Our own makings, Thou so generous in thy great-heart way.

The April 1927 number of *Music and Letters* was a special Beethoven issue and Gurney's contribution is clearly a transcript of his 'corrected' GMS text. Acknowledging receipt of the poem on 16 March 1927, A. H. Fox Strangways told Gurney that he had put it 'in a place of honour' and it was indeed printed, without a title and with minor changes in punctuation and spelling, as the first item in the issue.

There is a gap in line 19 between the words 'even' and 'to' in 1RVW, beside which Edmund Blunden has written 'Rasoumovsky' in pencil. Whilst the space could have conceivably contained the name of anything by Beethoven, the typist's inability to read Gurney's handwriting suggests an unfamiliar word and Blunden's annotation has accordingly been included, but in the spelling favoured by Gurney.

p.73   *Small Chubby Dams.* GMS64.3.34, *1954.80*, *1982.195*. GMS lacks line 11.

p.74   *Poets.* • GMS64.3.44, 1RVW16.81. GMS lacks line 5 and ends on the phrase 'degrees {to the lees.}' in line 17.

p.74   *June's Meadows.* • GMS64.3.15v, 1RVW16.82. GMS is called 'Haymaking' and lacks line 4.

p.75   *Roads — Those Roads.* GMS64.3.17, *1954.85*, *1973.126–127*, *1982.140*. This poem is called 'Roads' in both GMS and the index to the first version of *Rewards of Wonder*; GMS, in place of line 14, has: 'They call the mind to spaces and the width of {wide} sky.'

p.76   *Prelude (12/8 Time).* • GMS64.3.52v, 1RVW16.86.

p.76   *Deerhurst Church.* • GMS64.3.45v-46, 1RVW16.87. 'And where the slow cattle move with all valley slowness. | Such is Deerhurst, most noble, for the first time noble.' is inserted between lines 16 and 17 in GMS, which continues after line 23:

> It is true, for all its Nobleness of show and great plan.
> Deerhurst is of those things by the heart found wanting,
> Yet loved for disappointment like a strange woman,
> Who is kissed and desired, left and soon forgotten
> (Unless her will is recall) Anyway, always haunting.
> My mind that Church Deerhurst will be till there passes
> Some as strange cheat of beauty before my puzzling senses.
> So many things of different kinds, make haunting.

p.77   *Lovely Playthings.* LS64.12.2, EB64.12.1, GMS64.3.17v, *1954.81*, *1982.144*, *1996.22*, *1997.62*. LS lacks a title and has 'Dawn's banners spread and arch over in mystery,' in place of line 3 and 'After dawns pause — that halt — the slow moving of' for line 5.

p.78   *Late May.* • GMS64.3.18, *1934b.585*, **MMS64.11.134v**, 1RVW16.88.2. GMS has in place of lines 8 to 14: 'Then sees the light's flood in all-unimagined wonders — | Turns — chooses loveliest of dawn's changes.'

p.78   *Songs Come To The Mind.* GMS64.3.18v, 1RVW16.90, *1982.72*.

p.79   *Dawn.* • GMS64.3.19, 1RVW16.91. In place of lines 10 to 16, GMS has:

> The darkness, or above the darkened edge of the world ——
> Or the great flag of day even begun to be unfurled.

(Only a small pennon of honour in lovely manner)
The reward of work while others are in sleep still encircled.

p.79   *Buysscheure*. • GMS64.3.19v, **1RVW16.92**. This poem is called
'Windmills' in GMS and, in place of lines 3 to 14, has:

But Buysscheure's mill that might have whirled arms above
Soldiers of England long centuries ago in campaign proof —
I remember mist, because great St Omer gloomed
Magnificent with black smoke in a sunset — There boomed
And shouted colour and darkness in the sun's falling —
Colour was like a trumpet in the evening calling.
Spires and high places in a mixed glory glowed and gloomed . . . .
Buysscheure was a guard of wonder by luck called to honour.

p.80   *The Poet Walking*. GMS64.3.20, **1RVW16.93**, *1973.84*, *1982.83*. This
poem is called 'Recollection' in GMS and, in place of lines 5 to 17, has:

And they wonder at the Middle age
Tower tall —
Passed the Cross Roman
(Foundations hidden all)
To pass to the Dane ways —
And of later days —
Where Kineburgh's Cottage
Stands by other Cottages,
And if they felt the centuries to be
Sacred and all present as they were to me,
Then Europe blessed them with a loving touch —
And nothing much
Troubled them of poverty, or ~~incom~~ inconveniency,
Or of their unknown honour of manner,
Born of a City
Mixed of an old pride great Severn beside.
In a valley wide.
And Cotswold noble watching Wales — to Atlantic a guide.

p.81   *The   Comparison*.   PMS64.1.12,   PTS16.95,   **MMS64.11.135v**,
1RVW16.94, *1996.61*. PMS and PTS both lack the final stanza.

p.81   *Strange Hells*. PMS64.1.13, **MMS64.11.124v**, *1954.90*, *1982.140–141*,
1996.60. Because there are two surviving versions of 'Strange Hells' and
because both stem from the same manuscript source in PMS, they offer
a useful illustration of how Gurney revised his poems. Taking the
carbon-copy of PTS, now no longer extant, he replaced

And shames bitter as vermin and as silly
Peace does so bind and weaken with its carefully
And damnably constricting petty lengths
Of effort, hopelessly sweating out its strengths

In warm baths not in action, till the usual
And polite frame of human is filled full

with the line 'As one would have expected — the racket and fear guns made' and added lines 10 and 14. This text was then included in *Rewards of Wonder*. The ribbon-copy of PTS, again no longer extant, was repunctuated and later retyped as part of *Poems by Ivor Gurney (The Marbled Book, with later Additions)*.

p.82   *Crickley Morning.* • GMS64.3.41, 1RVW16.96. This poem is called 'Steel Light' in both GMS and the index to the first version of *Rewards of Wonder*; GMS, in place of lines 8 to 16, has:

Rosecoloured, ocean matching, and yet of the sky.
Nothing out of Shakespeare or loved Chaucer,
Milton or any other would fit my mood
So I mused desolately of music, and the one Master
Who exulted when Heaven so changed — whose adoring mood
Europe (after Her reflection) has honoured established good;
And went in to my room where the night-lamp, chaser
Of gloom for so many hours was not of longer need.
And opened shutters, saw the new day space stir ——
Life beginning a new day with a light in flood.

p.83   *Memory.* • GMS64.3.60v, 1RVW16.97. In place of lines 7 to 12, GMS has:

For all miracles happen of weather in this County ——
That has to call (Her hidden spirits) for more bounty,
And the gods give Her the pleasure of their largesse . . . . .
Shepherds warning; red sky; it may rain to day :
But a prayer of one small god in a lonely place,
Alone may keep all raininess or cloud-heaven away.

p.83   *That Centre of Old.* PMS64.1.14, 1RVW16.98, *1982.73*. PMS lacks lines 9, 15 and 20.

p.84   *Incredible Thing.* • PMS64.1.28v, PTS16.100, 1RVW16.99. PMS and PTS both end on line 8.

p.85   *Up Horsepools.* • PMS64.1.29v, PTS16.102, 1RVW16.101. PMS and PTS both end on line 12.

p.85   *Crickley.* • GMS64.3.28–29v, 1RVW16.103–104. Gurney's usual practice when correcting GMS in 1925 was to either delete or add material, but here he has divided his original text into three separate poems. The first poem, which retains the title 'Crickley', lacks lines 9 and 15 and ends with the line 'Butterflies are compared with afternoons hour by hour show.' and Gurney's signature, added after line 19. The second lacks a title and starts at line 20 with Gurney's replacement of 'There' with 'Of custom' to make a more striking opening, concluding after line 31 with the couplet 'Day in a grand arch makes it courses and upright {powers,} | Draws the full influence of all our poetries {into xi few magic hours.}'. The last is called 'Heights of the great Valley. (Crickley)' and follows on immediately, with the lines:

> Present to be there, to hover, and to be stable there
> In thousand ways ~~spa~~ shapes {out} conditions of rare
> Wonder, not else seen; ~~the~~ beautiful laving of light., clear light,
> Art's squarenesses build there, {(unconscious)} dramas {and} symphonies . . . . .

It lacks lines 42, 50, 51, 59 and 66 but includes an additional line — '(Crickley, standing above the unnoticing valley.)' — between lines 57 and 58.

p.88   *The Fatigue Party.* • GMS64.3.63, 1RVW16.105. In place of lines 8 to 17, GMS has:

> Mudsmears, Hell-disgust, and snipers — barrage-fears.
> When suddenly a voice swore an oath made me rejoice . . . .
> thinking of Shakespeare up in his place retired
> From London awhile, to what his heart desired,
> Country Company and talk earthy as red-earth's own . . . .
> A Verey light went up, and we huddled down.
> But I kept the memory of a phrase many a labourer he
> Must have used in anger, not knowing the Londoner,
> the gentleman play-writer was anyway near.
> Delighting me on Somme, as he by Windrush or dear
> Evenlode, so many centuries apart, the same thing known.

p.88   *Bacon of Mornings.* • GMS64.3.47, PMS64.1.18, 1RVW16.106. This poem is called 'First Thoughts' in GMS and, in place of lines 7 to 25, has:

> By Bourton or Stow, Rissingtons, Swells or Slaughters;
> (All clean thoughts, all of comrades or friendly daughters
> Of Cotswold, where the air makes plain goodness to man.)
> (All clean thoughts, the exile by his heart's love forsaken.)
> In the West Country, dawn-stir, here the hope of tea dear
> To every Gloucester heart; and it <u>may</u> be possible
> To dodge the bacon hunger with a draft of valour —
> Tea taken before the bacon has time to conquer.
> O Severn, O Cotswold, of Evenlode and tiny waters!

PMS lacks a title and, in place of lines 7 to 25, has:

> By Bourton or by Stow in the free morning —
> May-foam the high hills edge running adorning.
> But thats not yet, and bolts click, fingers bleed, curses
> Mutter and more, what fate, what disgustingness worse is
> Than this to be lying or standing in gray ditches,
> With rifle-grenades making whooshings and fitches.

And Goodness knows what unthought body creepings.
Planning dawn rising, snare-setting, and civil outrage
When Peace should pay the soldier life and wage;
Cotswold to be seeing, that edge of morning
Or Malvern of dark mornings heaving and frowning,
Guarding the north gates, as it were, upping-and-downing.

When a poem appears in both GMS and PMS, such as 'Half Dead' or
'Crucifix Corner', Gurney usually includes revised versions of both
texts in *Rewards of Wonder*. The non-appearance of a version of the
PMS text here is probably linked to it having been deleted with a single
diagonal line, resulting in it not even being typed out.

p.89   *The Soaking.* GMS64.3.47v, *1934a.203*, **1RVW16.107.2**, *1982.74*,
        1996.30.

p.90   *Merville.* • GMS64.3.48v, **1RVW16.108**. GMS ends on line 16.

p.90   *New Year's Eve.* GMS64.3.49, *1924a.234*, **1RVW16.109**, *1973.63*,
        1982.79–80, *1996.49*. In place of lines 14 to 18, GMS has:

> The North, and all Scott called me — Ballads and Burns again!
> Enough! I got up and lit (the last little bit
> but one) of candle and poked the remaining fire,
> Got some blaze into the cold; sat wrote verses there . . . .
> (Or music) "The Hundred pipers" had called so plain,
> ("And A'") and for three hours stuck it and worked as best
> Drippings, and cold, and misery would let desire.

1924a has instead: 'Here was no soul's cheat, friends were of love over
there — | How past thought, returning sweet! yet the soldier must
dare.'

p.91   *Robecq — A Memory.* • GMS64.3.50, **1RVW16.50**. This poem is called
        'To beat Gonnehem' in GMS and may be an attempt to better F. W.
        Harvey's 'Gonnehem', which Gurney greatly admired (Thornton 1991:
        529). However, not even the later addition of '(But Albert Church was
        noble too — for all its height hurt of gun batter.)' after line 10 has caused
        Gurney to amend his original judgement of '<u>unsuccessful</u>', written at
        the top of the page.

p.92   *Possessions.* GMS64.4.72v, *1934b.301*, **1RVW 16.111**, *1982.73–74,98*.
        GMS reads:

> Sand has the ants, clay ferny weeds for play
> But what shall please the wind now the trees are away
> War took on Witcombe steep?
> It breathes there, and wonders at old night roarings
> October time at all lights, and the new clearings
> For memory are like to weep.
> It was right for the beeches to stand over Witcombe reaches.
> until the wind roared and softened and died to sleep.

This text is a photocopy of half a page torn from a feint-ruled exercise book, the original fragment being now no longer extant. Although catalogued as being part of BMS, a more likely source is one of GMS's missing pages: the handwriting in the photocopy is closer to that of GMS than BMS and the last two lines of the text are clearly later additions, very similar in style to GMS's 1925 corrections. *1934b* ends on line 6.

p.92   *Billet.* GMS64.3.42, **1RVW 16.112**, *1982.74*. In place of lines 5 to 16, GMS has:

> Lovely overroofing worthy a king's cradling, —
> (This was at La Gorgues after a Hell unmatched
> Of strafe and strain) At La Gorgues we had the olden
> Mill to watch, and the estaminets where once one did
> Give a drink of cafè-au-lait fit for the first of Infantry,
> After Waterloo, Hastings, or any famous battle in fame.
> Rest after tiredness, good drink after the dixie-lid
> Steam, and the stillness and Hell-battering East of Laventie.

p.93   *Rouen.* • GMS64.3.50v, **1RVW 16.113**. In place of lines 11 to 13, GMS has: 'With a great rock like Gallipoli, of a newer renown.'

p.93   *Glimmering Dusk.* GMS64.3.51, **1RVW 16.114**, *1982.79*. In place of lines 8 to 11, GMS has:

> Of thought snatched ruthlessly, ~~a~~ punishingly, or worse."
> But the soul ~~of~~ amiable from the cool breathing of dusk
> ~~Burbled lovingly~~ {Talked to itself alone} of soft redressing ~~joys~~
>   {matters}
> And dragged that wounded unpitied hapless husk.
> That a kind law makes dust of at last and scatters.
> Paying the moments pain with Shakespeare odd fragments, or
> Such beauty as Marston or Cyril Tourneur utters.

p.94   *Friendly Are Meadows.* GMS64.3.52, *1954.82*, *1982.120, 236*. GMS lacks lines 13 to 14 and, in place of lines 17 to 20, has:

> Of world's binding, and {as not earth's} dust apart be loosed,
> And man's worship of all gray comforts ~~too~~ {be} abused,
> To ~~a~~ {mere} wonder at lightning and torrentous strong flying hail.

p.94   *Loam Lies Heavy.* • GMS64.3.54v, **1RVW 16.115**. In place of lines 9 and 10, GMS has:

> A not unpleasant dust, a not-too-shrunk-from
> Remain of ~~that~~ human ~~not~~ subject to common doom.
> But O that the lovely form with the shining eyes
> Which Orion and Argo might apprehend and Sirius
> Should ever fail to be mixed with any sort clays;
> Having seen all lights, adored, the most coloured or clearest,
> To lie (the case) where earth the mere glimmer of broken dark denies.

p.95   *Crucifix Corner.* GMS64.3.53v–54, GTS42.2.70, 1RVW16.116, *1973.57–58, 1996.61–62.* In place of line 25, GMS has:

> With joy above the sound of the pipes and the clarinets,
> the thought of Robert Burns drinking and talking his heart even,
> In late inns with good comrades, to all North gladness given.

p.96   *The Abbey.* • GMS64.3.58v–59, 1RVW16.117. In place of lines 8 to 21, GMS has:

> Of such should ever again come, (if the gods again are commanders)
>
> ——————
>
> And there find my comrades, and honourers, Roman sentinels,
> They all noble, I war poet and maker,
> Who would comfort pain long weighed on me (past human ills) ——
> And make me free again of every Cotswold acre.

p.96   *I Saw England (July Night).* BMS64.4.34, GMS64.3.55, 1RVW16.118, *1982.75, 1996.62.* BMS lacks a title and reads:

> I saw England
> And it was May dusk
> There were three aspens
> ~~Fair~~ Stiller none could ask
> Neither break nor trouble
> Slid out of them
> Arcturus Cor Caroli over
> Shone down dim.

In place of lines 9 to 17, GMS has:

> But I was alien ~~to~~ indeed, outwards I got driven,
> Yet despite all, given
> A ~~symbol~~ sign ~~of mis~~{un}doubtful of an England ~~I~~ {that} few
> Doubt, ~~fill~~ not many have seen,~~of~~
> ~~What~~ That Will Squele he knew
> And Edward Thomas was beloved of in cross ~~mood~~ {moods even.}

p.97   *First Time In.* GMS64.3.42v–43,44v–45,46v, 1RVW16.119–120, *1973.64–66, 1982.85–87.* In place of line 62, GMS has: 'Fritz strafed, our first strafe, rifle grenades and minniewerfers.' Pages 1 to 2v of PMS contains another version of this poem which, with minor revisions, was included in *Poems by Ivor Gurney (The Marbled Book, with later Additions).*

p.97   *The Unvisited Church.* • GMS64.3.60, 1RVW16.123. This poem is called 'A Church beside the Road.' in GMS and, in place of lines 12 to 19, has:

> That Severn churches all are places of worship (Save Cotswold) the
> flower
> And after all some man even as anxious as I
> To search out Gloucester, Her hidden and sacred beauty,

Many have gone with such desire to disappointments aware —
And praised alone a thought of accomplished Duty.
It was the builder failed for once and Gloucestershire.

p.99   *Brimscombe*.   GMS64.3.35v,   *1924a.237*,   **1RVW16.124**,   *1973.63*,
          1982.84, *1996.50*. 'Wonder of men had walked there, and old Romance'
          is inserted between lines 11 and 12 in GMS.

p.100   *Poem For End*. **1954.104**, *1973.130*, *1982.201–202*, *1996.63*. This is the
          only text in *Rewards of Wonder* with no extant manuscript source. Given
          that it closes this collection, it seems likely that the missing manuscript
          occupied a similar position in either PMS or GMS, both of which have
          had pages removed from the back of them.

Explanatory Notes

These notes offer a means by which the reader can make sense of Gurney's complex and often obscure system of allusion in *Rewards of Wonder*. References are given poem by poem in the order they appear in this edition, and those that appear more than once have been cross-referenced to the particular poem where their significance is greatest so as to avoid needless repetition. Annotations in arial refer to obscurities in variant texts in the green hardback manuscript notebook, detailed in the Textual Notes section.

Place-names whose meaning for Gurney is derived from either their personal or historical significance are explained here, whilst the remainder can be found on the maps which follow this section. These provide a useful means of understanding Gurney's personal geography. Not only do they enable the reader to locate the host of towns, villages and topographical features to which he alludes in *Rewards of Wonder*, but they also give a sense of the spatial reality underlying Gurney's poetic exploration of 'Cotswold, France, London' in this collection.

p.23   *The Lantern-Shine*. In April 1919, Gurney wrote to Marion Scott from Dryhill Farm, Shurdington: 'This is just, and just the place would please you! An old gray-stone rambling array of buildings under a Roman camp near a Roman villa where many things from time to time have been discovered' (Thornton 1991: 481).

p.23   *October*. **Equinoctial flood** the Severn Bore, a series of waves that rush upstream ahead of the tide on the River Severn, is at its most spectacular during the spring and autumn equinoxes in March and September. **diurnal** a term used in astronomy to mean 'occupying one day'. **turbid** muddy or thick. **Flat Holm** an island at the mouth of the Severn, six miles north-west of Weston-Super-Mare. **white tower** Gloucester Cathedral. **the Free States** the thirteen American states where slavery was banned prior to the Civil War of 1861–5. **Sagas** the Victorian enthusiasm for medieval Icelandic literature resulted in the publication of a great many translations of sagas in the nineteenth and early twentieth centuries. The Saga Library translations of William Morris and

Eiríkr Magnusson enjoyed a remarkable popularity and Gurney was familiar with at least one of the series — *The Story of Howard the Halt* (1891), a translation of *Hávarðar saga Ísfirðings* — which he described as 'not bad' (Thornton 1991: 530). **death songs of Dane** possibly a reference to 'The Musician's Tale — The Saga of King Olaf' by the American poet and essayist Henry Wadsworth Longfellow (1807–82). Published in the first part of his *Tales of a Wayside Inn* (1867), the poem tells the story of the eponymous hero's conflict with the Danes and climaxes with 'King Olaf's Death-Drink', in which Olaf defeats the Danes in a great battle before dying himself. In an asylum letter written in June 1925, Gurney reports having completed 'a great setting' of 'Olaf's Return' from the same work. **Gehenna** the Valley of Hinnom, near Jerusalem, where children were sacrificed to Moloch. II Kings 23:10 describes how this idolatry was abolished by Josiah during his religious reforms.

p.24   *Glory — and Quiet Glory.* **limns** an archiac term meaning 'paints' or 'depicts'. **Edward Thomas** Philip Edward Thomas (1878–1917), the English poet and essayist killed at the Battle of Arras on 9 April 1917. John Haines knew him well and it was he who initially stimulated Gurney's enthusiasm for Thomas's work. Gurney never met Thomas himself, but he was visited in Stone House by his widow Helen in 1932. **forty-eight Preludes and Fugues** see *Laventie Ridge* (p.136).

p.25   *Half Dead.* The 2/5th Gloucesters reached Caulaincourt on 30 March 1917 and because it was the only building in the village not to have been destroyed in the German retreat, two companies decided to risk the likelihood of booby-traps and sleep in the mausoleum. According to the Gloucesters' regimental history, 'it proved to be a precious uncomfortable dormitory and to have obtained any sleep on its draughty stone floor would have been an achievement beyond even the powers of the 2/5th Glosters' (Barnes 1930: 60). **Sirius** Alpha Canis Majoris, better known as the Dog Star, is the brightest star in the night sky. **Mars** the planet named after the Roman god of war. **Argo's stars** one of the brightest constellations in the Southern Region, named after the ship used by Jason in his search for the Golden Fleece. **the Sisters** the Pleiades, a constellation of seven stars in the Northern Region associated with rain and stormy weather. In Greek mythology, the Pleiades were the daughters of Atlas who were pursued by Orion until they translated themselves into the sky. **fatigue party** see *The Fatigue Party* (p.140). **Regulus** also known as 'The Ruler', this is one of the brightest stars in the Equatorial Region.

p.26   *Tobacco.* **Raleigh** Sir Walter Raleigh (1552–1618), the explorer and writer. He began the English colonisation of Virginia in 1584, introducing potatoes and tobacco to England on his return. **Verey lights**

flares fired from a special pistol, used for signalling at night or for illu-
minating the enemy's position. More usually spelt Very, after their
inventor Samuel W. Very. **Woodbines, Goldflakes** untipped ciga-
rettes issued to soldiers in plentiful quantities. **sly fatigue parties** see
The Fatigue Party (p.140). **Aeneas' sailors** see 'Virgil' in *Crickley*
(p.139). **Irus** see 'Homer' in *Sheer Falls of Green Slope* (p.136). **the
legions Germanicus met** Germanicus Julius Caesar (15 BC–AD 19),
the Roman military commander who was nephew of the Emperor
Tiberius and father of Caligula. When legions stationed in Germany
mutinied in AD14, it was he who restored order and quelled the uprising.
pipe, and tabor a pair of Elizabethan instruments designed to be
played together by one person. **Daniel** Samuel Daniel (1562–1619), the
poet, essayist and masque writer best known for his *Defence of Rhyme*
(1602) and *Hymen's Triumph* (1615).

p.28   *Leckhampton Elbow.* Leckhampton Hill was the site of extensive quar-
rying during the eighteenth and nineteenth centuries. It became a
popular weekend attraction for residents of Cheltenham and Gloucester
on account of the Devil's Chimney, a prominent pillar of stone deliber-
ately carved out of the sheer cliff edge at Leckhampton Hill by quar-
rymen. **kite** see *Crickley* (p.139).

p.29   *Tobacco.* See *Tobacco* (p.126). **Minnie-werfer** a German trench-mortar
whose name literally means 'bomb thrower'.

p.30   *Queen of Cotswold.* Cotswold wool was a highly prized export in Europe
in the Middle Ages and various towns in Gloucestershire thrived on the
industry. Gurney is here most likely referring to Chipping Camden,
whose town hall, market hall, wool church and almshouses were all built
by prosperous medieval and Elizabethan wool merchants.

p.31   *By Severn.* **Oriana's playwrights** Oriana was one of the names by
which Elizabethan poets referred to Elizabeth I. **Elizabethans of
Thames, South and Northern side** presumably playwrights, as most
of the Elizabethan playhouses were located on the banks of the Thames.
The frontispiece of the Mermaid series, which reprinted 'The Best
Plays of the Old Dramatists', was an engraving of the Bankside and its
theatres and may have been Gurney's inspiration here. **meeding** an
archaism meaning 'rewarding' or 'praising'.

p.32   *The Tax Office.* Gurney began work at the Gloucester Tax Office in
College Court on 3 July 1922. In a letter to Marion Scott, he describes
the building as 'quite a fine building with something of a staircase, and
a view across to Malvern from higher window looks, and an interesting
view across good slate roofs and honest 18th Century brick. The front is
very fine Corinthian (or sort of) with well spaced windows. It is not so
bad for Taxes; from which I have cribbed the best of Poetry Note Books'
(Thornton 1991: 540). He lost his job there after twelve weeks.

Waltheof or Egbert see *The Bargain* (p.135).

p.33   *Praise of Tobacco*. **Great Jonson** see *If Ben Jonson Were Back* (p.136).
Charlemagne Charlemagne (742–814) was the legendary king of the
Franks celebrated in the medieval French epic, the *Chanson de Roland*.
Gurney knew the poem in C. K. Scott Moncrieff's 1919 translation and
managed to obtain Scott Moncrieff's autograph for F. W. Harvey's
sister (Thornton 1991: 505). **precedition** Gurney's own coinage,
meaning 'the act of going before'. **Scott** see 'Sir Walter' in *Crucifix
Corner* (p.134). **Hardy** Thomas Hardy (1840–1928), the poet and
novelist. Gurney greatly admired *The Dynasts* (1908), describing 'the
whole characterisation and some of the scenes' as 'colossally good'
(Thornton 1991: 7). **Belloc** Hilaire Belloc (1870–1953), the essayist,
poet and travel writer. Gurney called his travel book *The Path to Rome*
(1902) 'my trench companion' and dedicated *Severn & Somme* to Belloc
because of his affection for it (Thornton 1987: 19). **Bach** see *Laventie
Ridge* (p.136). **Brahms** Johannes Brahms (1833–97), the German
composer best known for *Ein Deutsches Requiem* (1868). **Beethoven** see
Thoughts on Beethoven (p.137). **Carlyle** Thomas Carlyle (1795–1881),
the essayist and political philosopher whose works include *Sartor
Resartus* (1834) and *Past and Present* (1843). **ruth** see *The Unvisited
Church* (p.142). **Epigrams** see *If Ben Jonson Were Back* (p.136).

p.34   *Laventie*. **the Line** a military term describing the arrangement of
trenches on the Western Front. Troops spent between three and seven
days in the Front or First Line trench, which directly faced the enemy.
They would then withdraw to the Support Line trench for a similar
period of time and then go back to the Reserve Line trench. After this a
week was spent 'on Rest' before returning to the Front. **Australian
gunners** the 5th Australian Division was stationed at Laventie during
the summer of 1916. It played a major part in the fighting around
Aubers Ridge in late July, an action where the 2/5th Gloucesters were
held in reserve. **café-au-lait** tinned coffee, made with milk. **dugout**
the military term for a roofed shelter in the trenches, also ironically
known as a 'funk-hole'. **Tommies** the traditional nickname for the
British soldier derived from 'Thomas Atkins', the name used in spec-
imen official forms in the early nineteenth century. **minnie-werfs** see
Tobacco (p.127). **Australian miners** the Australian Mining Corps
spent much of July 1916 preparing the 'Red Lamp' detonation near the
Line at Laventie. **strafes** sustained bombardments by rifle or artillery,
from the German *Gott strafe England* — 'God punish England'.
**Maconachie, Paxton, Tickler, and Gloucester's Stephens | Fray
Bentos, Spiller and Baker** all types of food issued as rations in the
trenches. Maconachie, for example, was a tinned meat and vegetable
mixture, consisting largely of carrots and turnips in gravy, whilst Fray

Bentos was the most common brand of corned beef or 'Bully'. Both Tickler's and Stephens were brands of jam, the latter being particularly significant for Gurney because it was made in Gloucester and the fact that Basil Cridlan, his army companion, had worked as an analyst at the Stephens factory before the war (Thornton 1991: 49). **Citron** a French lemon drink made from cordial. **Grenadine** a French alcoholic cordial made from the syrup of pomegranates.

p.36   *The Ford.* Henry V (1387–1422) invaded France on 13 August 1415 and besieged Harfleur, finally capturing it two months later. Heavily depleted and racked with dysentry and other illnesses, the British army then marched south, crossing the River Somme at the fords at Voyenne and Béthencourt on 19 October, and went on to defeat the French at Agincourt on 25 October. Shakespeare celebrates this campaign in *Henry V* (1600) and, in 1917, the 2/5 Gloucesters found themselves retracing Henry's route under similar conditions as they followed the German retreat.

p.36   *The Bargain.* **Carthage should be rased** see 'Cato' in *Roman, and the War Poet* (p.133). **Drake** Francis Drake (*circa* 1550–96), the seaman and explorer who played an instrumental part in the defeat of the Spanish Armada in 1588. **Hawkins** Sir John Hawkins (1532–95), the sailor and slave trader who helped to defeat the Spanish Armada in 1588. **drouth** dry weather or drought.

p.38   *The Ford.* **perry** a cider made from pears.

p.39   *The Touchstone (Watching Malvern).* **Bear** Ursa Major, the constellation in the Northern Region whose seven brightest stars form the Plough. **the Pole** the Pole Star or, to use its proper name, Polaris. **Paul's** St Paul's Cathedral, at the top of Ludgate Hill. It was reconstructed in 1669 by Sir Christopher Wren (1632–1723) after the Fire of London. **Fleet** both river and street, leading up Ludgate Hill to St Paul's Cathedral.

p.39   *Thoughts of New England.* **Kineburgh's cottage** see 'Peter's Abbey' below. **Raven Tavern** a sixteenth-century inn in Hare Lane which was owned by the Hoare family, some of whom emigrated to America with the Pilgrim Fathers in the *Mayflower* in 1620. *Captains Courageous* see 'where Kipling loved and ranged' below. **Whitman** Walt Whitman (1819–92), the poet whose verse was collected in the final edition of *Leaves of Grass* (1889). Gurney frequently refers to individual poems such as 'This Compost' (1871) and 'Song of Myself', which was the untitled introduction to the first edition of *Leaves of Grass* (1855), and he also alludes to larger works such as *Drum-Taps* (1865) and *Specimen Days and Collect* (1882), Whitman's prose account of his experiences as a nurse during the American Civil War. **Huck Finn's cavern** One of Gurney's favourite American novels was *The Adventures of Huckleberry*

Finn (1884) by Samuel Clemens (1835–1910), better known as Mark Twain. Here, he refers to the cave discovered by Huck and Jim during their adventures on Jackson's Island in Chapter IX. **Citizen** *The Citizen* and *The Gloucester Journal* were Gurney's two local newspapers. **Thoreau** Henry David Thoreau (1817–62), the poet, travel writer and essayist whose works include *Walden* (1854) and *Excursions* (1863). *Evangeline* **Evangeline** (1847), by the American poet and essayist Henry Wadsworth Longfellow (1807–82), is a narrative poem set in the early years of the American nation. **Domesday Book** despite the monastery of St Peter having fallen into disrepair, it was in the Chapter House there that William I held court during Christmas 1085 and planned the preparation of the Domesday Book. The core of the present building is the nave consecrated in 1100, where the coronation of the boy king Henry V took place in 1216. **four ways** Gloucester's four principal roads are Northgate Street, Southgate Street, Eastgate Street and Westgate Street. They meet at the centre of the town, where a medieval cross stood until 1751. **Abana and Pharpar** 'Are not Abana and Pharpar, rivers of Damascus, better than all the waters of Israel?' (II Kings 5:12). **Washington** George Washington (1732–99), commander of the American forces during the War of Independence and President of America from 1789 to 1797. **Lincoln** Abraham Lincoln (1800–65), President of America from 1861 until his assassination in 1865. **Lowell** James Russell Lowell (1819–91), the poet and essayist whose works include *The Biglow Papers* (1848 and 1867) and *My Study Windows* (1871). **Hawthorne** Nathaniel Hawthorne (1804–64), the novelist best known for *The Scarlet Letter* (1850), *The House of the Seven Gables* (1851) and *Tanglewood Tales* (1861). **Holmes** Oliver Wendell Holmes (1809–94), the poet and essayist whose works include *The Autocrat of the Breakfast-Table* (1858) and *Songs of Many Seasons* (1875). **the Wilderness** State capital of Virginia until 1779 and scene of a Civil War battle in 1864. **Richmond** Richmond Heights was the scene of two battles during the American Civil War, in 1862 and later in 1865 when the town was besieged by the Federals. **Chattanooga's thronged woods** the scene of two major Civil War battles in 1863. **Peter's Abbey** the site of Gloucester Cathedral was occupied during the Dark Ages by the Benedictine monastery of St Peter, founded by King Osric in AD 681 and run by his sister Kyneburg. Kyneburg was remembered in 1559, when Sir Thomas Bell founded an almshouse called St Kineburgh's Hospital within the cathedral precincts. **where Kipling loved and ranged** Rudyard Kipling (1865–1936), the poet, novelist and author of short stories whose *Captains Courageous* (1897), a novel of sea adventure, and *Puck of Pook's Hill* (1906) — 'Sussex tales out of Roman heights callen' — were much admired by Gurney. Kipling

EXPLANATORY NOTES 131

describes his experiences in New England in 1892 in *Something of Myself* (1936). **Grant's men** Ulysses Simpson Grant (1822–85), Commander-in-Chief of the Federal forces during the American Civil War and President of America between 1869 and 1877. **Lee's men** General Robert E. Lee (1807–70), Commander-in-Chief of the Confederate forces in the American Civil War when the final surrender was made at Appomattox in 1865. **Crecy window** the east window of Gloucester Cathedral, known locally as the Creçy window, was constructed between 1347 and 1350 to commemorate the Battle of Creçy in 1346.

p.42   *When The Sun Leaps Tremendous.* **Orion** the constellation in the Equatorial Region which represents the famous giant and hunter. **Arcturus** one of the brightest stars in the Equatorial Region, which can be seen from everywhere on Earth except Antarctica. **the Great Bear** see 'Bear' in *The Touchstone (Watching Malvern)* (p.129).

p.43   *Canadians.* Gurney might here be describing an encounter with the Newfoundland Regiment, almost completely destroyed in the Battle of the Somme, but these Canadians are more probably men from the 1st and 2nd Divisions of the Canadian Corps, who were involved in heavy fighting in the Thiepval area in the second half of 1916. **billets** see *Billet* (p.141). **Death's Valley** Death Valley — 'that cheerful spot appropriately named' (Barnes 1930: 54) — was the section of the trench system closest to the British Front Line at Grandecourt, so called because of its resemblance to 'the valley of the shadow of death' in Psalms 23:4. **Stewart White** Stewart White (1873–1946), the Canadian author of popular novels depicting rugged outdoor life such as *The Claim Jumpers* (1901) and *The Blazed Trail* (1902). **Jack London** Jack London (1878–1916), the novelist and travel writer best known for *The Call of the Wild* (1903), *White Fang* (1906) and *John Barleycorn* (1913).

p.45   *The Ford.* See *The Ford* (p.129).

p.45   *Laventie Front.* See *Laventie* (p.128). **Noman's** No Man's Land is the military term for the space between opposing trenches. Gurney's spelling is unusual but is also used, for example, by Henry Williamson in *A Fox Under My Cloak* (1955). **minnie-werfers** see *Tobacco* (p.127).

p.47   *Cyril Tourneur.* Cyril Tourneur (*circa* 1575–1626), the dramatist whose works include *The Revenger's Tragedy* (1607) and *The Atheist's Tragedy* (1611). **Southwark** the borough at the south end of London Bridge, famous as the site of ancient inns and theatres such as the Globe, the Hope and the Rose. **Daniel** see *Tobacco* (p.127). **Juliet** the eponymous heroine of Shakespeare's *Romeo and Juliet* (1595). **Greene** Robert Greene (1560–92), the poet, playwright and pamphleteer, whose works include *A Groat's Worth of Wit Bought with a Million of Repentance* (1592) and *Friar Bacon and Friar Bungay* (1594). **Celia** possibly the daughter of Duke Frederick in Shakespeare's *As You Like It* (1598), but more probably the persecuted wife of Corvino in Ben Jonson's *Volpone* (1605). **Jonson's Fulvia** see *If Ben Jonson Were Back* (p.136). **Lamb** Charles Lamb (1775–1884), the playwright, essayist and poet. His *Specimens of English Dramatic Poets who lived about the time of Shakespeare* (1808) contains substantial extracts from Tourneur's *The Atheist's Tragedy*, *The Drowned Soldier* and *The Revenger's Tragedy*. **"cloth of silver" clothes the word "slut" for ever** Gurney was evidently much taken by Vendice's speech in Act IV, Scene 4 of Tourneur's *The Revenger's Tragedy*: 'The Duke's son's great concubine! | A drab of state, a cloth o'silver slut, | To have her train borne up and her soul | Trail i' the dirt!' as a letter of 1922 to Edward Marsh shows (Thornton 1991: 526–7).

p.48   *First March.* Gurney wrote to Marion Scott on 27 March 1917 during the German retreat: 'On the march not many days ago we passed a ruined garden, and there were snowdrops, snowdrops, the first flowers my eyes had seen for long. So I plucked one each for my friends that I so desire to see again, and one for Gloucestershire . . . .' (Thornton 1991: 236). **Winter Tale touch** Shakespeare's *The Winter's Tale* (1611) is noted for its magical transformations and miraculous rebirths. **Bach fugue wonder** see *Laventie Ridge* (p.136).

p.49   *Of Bricks and Brick Pits.* **the Siege** Gloucester took the side of Parliament during the English Civil War and withstood a month-long siege by Royalist forces in 1643. **Westgate Street** one of Gloucester's four principal roads. **squattering** a dialect term meaning 'fluttering or struggling among water or soft mud'.

p.50   *Cotswold Slopes.* **sorners** Scots slang for persons who impose upon others for their bed and board. **Thebes** the ancient capital of Egypt. **strength of Timgad** the building of Timgad in North Africa was influenced by the Roman architect Vitruvius Pollio.

p.51   *Robecq.* **All Hallows** 1 November. The feast day for the commemoration of all saints known in French as *Toussaints*.

p.51   *Near Vermand.* **Bach** see *Laventie Ridge* (p.136).

p.52   *At the Inn.* **vamp** where a pianist improvises an accompaniment around three simple key chords. **frowardly** an archaic term for 'perversely'. **'Widdicombe Fair'** a popular folksong from Somerset which tells the story of Tom Pearce's grey mare and 'Uncle Tom Cobleigh and all'. Gurney's wartime nickname of 'Peter' was derived from the Peter Gurney mentioned in the refrain of this song (Thornton 1991: 183). **'I'm Seventeen Come Sunday'** a folksong from Somerset which tells the story of a soldier's love for a 'fair pretty maid', used by Ralph Vaughan Williams in his *English Folk Song Suite* (1923). **'Furze'** better known as 'The Furze Field', this folksong collected in Hampshire in

1907 uses allusions to country sports to refer to sexual matters. **'Spanish Sailors'** also known as 'The Spanish Ladies', this sea-shanty features a group of sailors bidding 'Farewell and Adieu to you, fair Spanish Ladies' as they sail for home. **Bardolph** Falstaff's drinking companion in Shakespeare's *Henry IV* (1558–1600), *Henry V* (1600) and *The Merry Wives of Windsor* (1602). **Drayton** Michael Drayton (1563–1631), the poet whose fame rests upon his *Poems Lyrick and Pastoral* (1605) and his great poem on the landscape and history of Britain, *Poly-Olbion* (1622). **'Golden Vanity'** a traditional English ballad concerning the death of a cabin boy off the coast of 'the Low-lands low'. **Shallow** a foolish country Justice in Shakespeare's *Henry IV, Part 2* (1600). **Will Squele** see *I Saw England (July Night)* (p.141).

p.53   *Of Trees Over There.* **All Souls** 2 November. The feast day intended for the mitigation by prayer of the suffering of souls in Purgatory.

p.54   *Gifts and Courtesy.* **fatigues** see *The Fatigue Party* (p.140). **Hugo's pages** Victor Hugo (1802–85), the French poet and novelist best known for his novels *Notre Dame de Paris* (1831) and *Les Misérables* (1862). **Welsh regiment who took us in** see *First Time In* (p.141). **bully** the soldier's nickname for tinned corned beef. **Somme Farm** a noted landmark on the Ypres salient.

p.53   *Roman, and the War Poet.* **Plutarch** Plutarch (*circa* AD 46–120), the Greek philosopher and biographer best known for his forty-six *Lives* of Greek and Roman statesmen and soldiers. Gurney recommended him to Herbert Howells as part of 'a pretty complete diet' in July 1916 (Thornton 1991: 72). **Antony** Marcus Antonius (*circa* 80–32 BC), the Roman statesman and soldier whose infatuation with Cleopatra led to his downfall. Gurney was familiar with at least two versions of Antony's life through his reading of Plutarch and Shakespeare's *Antony and Cleopatra* (1606). **Beethoven the Roman** see *Thoughts on Beethoven* (p.137). **Jonson** see *If Ben Jonson were Back* (p.136). **Cato** Marcus Porcius Cato (234–149 BC), the Roman statesman known as 'The Censor' because of his austerity and puritanism. According to Plutarch, his suspicion of Hellenism led him to end his speeches with the phrase *Delenda est Carthago* — 'Carthage must be destroyed'. **Brutus** Marcus Junius Brutus (85–42 BC), the Roman politician and soldier best remembered for his part in the assassination of Julius Caesar. Again, Gurney's knowledge of him comes from Plutarch and Shakespeare, in this case *Julius Caesar* (1599). **Maximus** Fabius Maximus Verrucosus Cunctator (*circa* 275–203 BC), the Roman general and statesman known as 'The Delayer' because of his tactic of avoiding open warfare with the Carthaginians during the Second Punic War. Gurney was familiar with Plutarch's account of his life. **my wounded arm** Gurney was shot in the upper arm during a night attack at Vermand on 7 April 1917.

134   EXPLANATORY NOTES

Marion Scott records that 'when he saw a German under a tree just
about to shoot him, he could barely fling the bomb that saved his own
life. He just did it, but was shot in the shoulder' (Scott 1938: 5).

p.55   *Kilns*. **meres** the Old English term for lakes or ponds. **Domesday** see
'Domesday Book' in *Thoughts of New England* (p.129).

p.57   *Riez Bailleul*. **Sirius** see *Half Dead* (p.126). **the Line** see *Laventie*
(p.128). **estaminet** a French café selling food and alcohol.

p.58   *Riez Bailleul Also*. **billets** see *Billet* (p.141). **dixies** the military term for
a large iron pot used by soldiers for cooking and brewing tea. **Lights-
Out** a bugle call used to signal the end of the military day.

p.58   *What I Will Pay*. **Beethoven** see *Thoughts on Beethoven* (p.137). **Bach**
see *Laventie Ridge* (p.136). **Jonson** see *If Ben Jonson were Back* (p.136).
lave a poeticism for 'bathe'. **Carlyle** see *Praise of Tobacco* (p.128).
Borrow see 'dear *Lavengro* recalling thus' in *Deerhurst Church* (p.138).
Homer see *Sheer Falls of Green Slope* (p.136).

p.59   *Smudgy Dawn*. **fire-swinger** the sun.

p.60   *Crucifix Corner*. There were at least two landmarks on the Western
Front nicknamed 'Crucifix Corner'. Gurney is referring here to a junc-
tion of the trench system on the banks of the Ancre near Aveluy, named
after the dismembered crucifix that stood there. Gurney spent
Christmas 1916 at the 61st Divisional Headquarters at Aveluy, along-
side troops from a variety of Highland regiments such as the 6th and 7th
Black Watch, the 5th and 6th Seaforths and the 7th Argyll and
Sutherlands. He became friendly with the pioneers of the 8th Royal
Scots Regiment, writing to Marion Scott that 'the Scots are certainly the
finest of races, and the hardiest' (Thornton 1991: 176). **chlorinated
clay mixture** chlorine was used to purify water supplies on the
Western Front. **billets** see *Billet* (p.141). **crump** the burst from a 5.9
inch shell, derived from the sound it made on impact. **last Trump** 'In
a moment, in the twinkling of an eye, at the last trump; for the trumpet
shall sound and the dead shall be raised incorruptible, and we shall be
changed' (I Corinthians 15:52). **'Hundred Pipers and A"** a traditional
Scots song, with modern words by Lady Nairne, used as a marching
song by Scottish regiments. **'Happy we've been a' tegether'** a senti-
mental Scottish folksong popular amongst Highland regiments during
the Great War. **Orion** see *When The Sun Leaps Tremendous* (p.131).
seven stars see 'the Sisters' in *Half Dead* (p.126). **Sir Walter** Sir
Walter Scott (1771–1832), the Scottish novelist and poet whose works
include *The Antiquary* (1816) and *Midlothian* (1818). Gurney elsewhere
associates him with Perthshire because many of his novels, such as
Waverley (1816) and *Rob Roy* (1817), are set in that part of Scotland.
Redgauntlet **bringing Solway clear to the mind** part of the action in
Scott's *Redgauntlet* (1824), a historical novel depicting Bonnie Prince

Charlie's return, takes place in the Solway Firth area.

p.61   *Half Dead.* see *Half Dead* (p.126).

p.62   *First Time In.* see *First Time in* (p.141). **the Line** see *Laventie* (p.128).
Ulysses see 'Homer' in *Sheer Falls of Green Slope* (p.136).

p.63   *The Song.* **'High Germany'** a popular Somerset ballad telling the story
of thwarted love during the Napoleonic Wars, used by Ralph Vaughan
Williams in his *English Folk Song Suite* (1923) and Gustav Holst in *A
Somerset Rhapsody* (1910). **'I'm only Ninety-Eight'** perhaps a music-
hall song, although Ralph Vaughan Williams collected a folksong about
a youth pressed in naval service called 'On Board the Ninety-Eight' in
Norfolk in 1905 and later incorporated it into his *Norfolk Rhapsody in E
Minor* (1906). **'Widdicombe Fair'** see *At The Inn* (p.132). **Mile End's-
Holloway's favourite drolleries** a reference to the comic songs
popular in the music halls of London's East End. **the Line** see *Laventie*
(p.128). **Plumstead's delight** Gurney's familiarity with entertain-
ments in this part of London's East End stems from the two weeks he
spent playing the piano in a cinema there in January 1922 (Thornton
1991: 522–523). **orts** a Middle English word meaning refuse scraps or
left-overs. **'The Blacksmith's Song'** either 'Twankydillo', a Cavalier
song praising 'the jolly blacksmith', or 'A Blacksmith Courted Me', the
folksong collected by Ralph Vaughan Williams in Herefordshire in 1909
and used as the basis for his setting of the hymn 'He who would valiant
be'. **'Farmer's Boy'** a folksong collected in Yorkshire with the chorus:
'To reap and sow | To plough and mow | to be a farmer's boy'.

p.64   *La Gorgues.* **fatigues** see *The Fatigue Party* (p.140). **Line trouble** see
Laventie (p.128). **Gloucester's B Company** the company of the 2/5th
Gloucesters to which Gurney belonged until his transfer to the 184
Machine Gun Company on 15 July 1917. **café-au-lait** see *Laventie*
(p.128).

p.65   *Northleach.* **Drayton's hour** see 'Drayton' in *At The Inn* (p.132).

p.67   *Blighty.* **Blighty** pre-war soldiers' slang for home or England derived
from *bilayati*, the Hindustani word for foreigner. A wound which
ensured evacuation to England was known as 'a blighty one' and gave
rise to the term 'lucky blighter'.

p.67   *The Bargain.* Gurney's references to Waltheof, the Abbot of Stare, the
Mill of Knut's Weald, Egbert and Hugo in *Rewards of Wonder* may be
derived from one of the antiquaries celebrated in 'June's Meadows'. In
October 1920, for example, he mentions discovering Rudge's
Agricultural Survey of Gloucestershire (1807) for '2/6 I think' (Thornton
1991: 505) and he may have been familiar with others, such as Samuel
Rudder's *A New History of Gloucestershire* (1779) or Samuel Lysons' *A
Collection of Gloucestershire Antiquities* (1803). On the other hand, the
names Cnut, Egbert, Hugo and Waltheof all appear in different contexts

136 EXPLANATORY NOTES

in the *Anglo-Saxon Chronicle* and it may be that Gurney borrowed them from either E. E. C. Gomme's 1909 translation or, more probably, the pre-war Everyman edition of the Rev. James Ingram's translation.

p.68   *Laventie Ridge.* An echo of Gurney's earlier 'Bach and the Sentry', written at Laventie in 1916 and published in *Severn & Somme* (Thornton 1987: 29). Gurney's enthusiasm for Johann Sebastian Bach (1685–1750) is evident from his letters and was particularly centred on *Das Wohltemperirte Klavier*. Also known as 'the 48', this consists of two sets of preludes and fugues in every minor and major key and Gurney frequently recommends individual preludes from this work to friends in his wartime correspondence.

p.69   *Sheer Falls of Green Slope.* **Aeschylus** Aeschylus (525–456 BC), the Athenian tragic poet. Gurney read and admired John Stuart Blackie's translation of *The Lyrical Dramas of Aeschylus* (1906) in the trenches, writing to Marion Scott: '"Agamemnon" is very fine, and the man does know how to translate' (Thornton 1991: 160). **Sophocles** Sophocles (*circa* 496–406 BC), the Athenian tragic poet and dramatist. Only seven of the 123 plays he wrote survive, including *Antigone, King Oedipus, Oedipus at Colonus* and *Electra*. Reading his plays in June 1921, Gurney judged him 'at present' to be 'better than *Prometheus Unbound*' (Thornton 1991: 516). **Homer** Homer (*circa* 9th century BC), the Greek epic poet. Gurney read *The Iliad* in the Bohn edition, which reprinted George Chapman's 1611 translation (Thornton 1991: 525) and it is likely that he was also familiar with Chapman's version of *The Odyssey*. Odysseus — known in Latin as Ulysses — was the mythical king who spent twenty years, many of them at sea, attempting to return home to Ithaca after the Trojan Wars. Upon his arrival, he discovers his wife, Penelope, is besieged by suitors and so disguises himself as a beggar to keep watch over her. He encounters the scornful beggar Arnaeus, also known as Irus because he carries out the commissions of Penelope's suitors, in Book XI, and a fight between the two men results in Odysseus felling him with a single blow.

p.70   *If Ben Jonson Were Back.* Ben Jonson (1572–1637), the poet and dramatist whose works include *Volpone* (1605), *Catiline* (1611) and *The Alchemist* (1610). Gurney admired Jonson for his military service in Flanders, where he allegedly killed a Spaniard in single combat, and his stubborn belief in his own superior talent and he celebrates both the man and his work in many of his poems. Here, he alludes to *Catiline* — Fulvia is the mistress of the disgraced Senator, Curius, in this play — and Face's speech on the delights of Drugger's tobacco in Act III, Scene 1 of *The Alchemist* and also Jonson's verse collections *The Forest* — his 'Commematory verses' — and *Epigrams*, first published in the Folio *Works* of 1616. Gurney associates him with the Firth of Forth because of the time he spent at Hawthornden, visiting his fellow poet William Drummond (1585–1649). **Smithfield** a market-place and parade ground north-west of the river Thames. It was here that Richard II met Wat Tyler in 1381 and was later used as a site for the public burning of heretics. **Tothill** Tothill Fields in Westminster was used as a place for archery practice in Elizabethan times. **Fleet** see *The Touchstone (Watching Malvern)* (p.129). **Southwark** see *Cyril Tourneur* (p.131). **Paul's** see *The Touchstone (Watching Malvern)* (p.129). **fopling** a dandy. **gulls** Elizabethan slang for persons who are easily fooled.

p.71   *Tewkesbury.* **tilth** an area of cultivation, from the Old English *tilthe*. **morrice** more usually spelt 'morris', this is the form of traditional country dance preserved and popularised by Cecil Sharpe's English Folk Dance Society in the early years of the twentieth century. **Lucy** a prominent family of Stratford landowners and the inhabitants of Charlecote Manor since the twelfth century. According to legend, it was being caught by Sir Thomas Lucy poaching deer in the grounds that caused the young Shakespeare to move to London to become an actor. **Gloucester's near doom** see 'the Siege' in *Of Bricks and Brick Pits* (p.132).

p.72   *Thoughts on Beethoven.* It is not clear which of Gurney's friends first encouraged his enthusiasm for Ludwig van Beethoven (1770–1827), although 'The First Violets' in *Best poems* suggests that it was Margaret Hunt, his friend from Gloucester (Thornton & Walter 1995: 45–46). Another possibility is Marion Scott, whose study of the composer, *Beethoven*, was published in 1934. The *Rasumovsky Quartets* Op.59, composed in 1806 and dedicated to the Russian ambassador to Vienna, Count Rasumovsky, were a particular favourite of Gurney's and his allusion to 'Beethoven the Roman' is either a reference to another work, the *Concerto No. 5 for Piano and Orchestra in E Flat Major*, also known as the *Emperor*, or an acknowledgement of the 'square making' in Beethoven's compositions that Gurney elsewhere associated with the Romans. **Homer** see *Sheer Falls of Green Slope* (p.136). **Ben Jonson** see *If Ben Jonson Were Back* (p.136). **Aeschylus** see *Sheer Falls of Green Slope* (p.136).

p.73   *Small Chubby Dams.* **sprackly** dialect for 'actively' or 'smartly'. **Brahms** see *Praise of Tobacco* (p.128).

p.74   *Poets.* **Eridanus** a winding constellation of almost three hundred stars in the Southern Region, named after a mythological river. **Ben Jonson** see *If Ben Jonson Were Back* (p.136).

p.74   *June's Meadows.* **the Golden Age** see *First Time In* (p.141). **the antiquary** see *The Bargain* (p.135).

p.75   *Roads — Those Roads.* **the Abbey** see 'Peter's Abbey' in *Thoughts of New England* (p.129).

138   EXPLANATORY NOTES

p.76   *Prelude (12/8 Time).* **12/8 Time** a fast compound quadruple time
        signature, consisting of four dotted crotchets to a bar.

p.76   *Deerhurst Church.* Gurney first visited the church of St Mary at
        Deerhurst in May 1922: 'Yesterday afternoon I went to Deerhurst for
        my first time. The Saxon chapel is nothing but the Norman and later
        church was very interesting with a tall oblong tower, graceful and strong
        and some of the finest carved doorways you could wish to see.'
        (Thornton 1991: 533). Although possessing a monastery and chapel in
        pre-Norman times, the village is not mentioned in the Domesday Book.
        dear *Lavengro* **recalling thus** a curious reference to George Borrow
        (1803–81), the novelist and essayist whose works, based on his travels,
        include *The Bible in Spain* (1843) and *Wild Wales* (1862). His autobio-
        graphical novel *Lavengro* (1851) tells the story of the wanderings of a
        soldier's son across Britain and Europe but there is no clear connection
        between this text and the village of Deerhurst. Gurney may have in
        mind the opening of the novel, where Borrow rhapsodises upon 'pretty,
        quiet D ——', or the passage in Chapter VIII of *The Romany Rye*
        (1857), the sequel to *Lavengro*, where Borrow talks of 'the old church of
        pretty D ——' but Borrow is referring to his birthplace of East
        Dereham in Norfolk in both cases.

p.78   *Late May.* **Helen in the north** possibly a reference to 'Helen of
        Kirconnell', a traditional Scottish ballad. In a letter to Marion Scott of
        July 1916 Gurney writes: 'you said some time ago, that "Helen of
        Kirconnell" would do well to set. She is a fine wench but too long and
        repetitious and her limbs too much in evidence to be easy in surrender'
        (Thornton 1991: 115). No setting of this poem survives and it may be
        that Annie Nelson Drummond is the Helen in the North that Gurney
        has in mind. **Forth** see *If Ben Jonson Were Back* (p.136). **Hebrides** the
        Hebrides Overture by Felix Mendelssohn (1809–47). *The book of Five
        makings* contains two poems inspired by the piece (Thornton & Walter
        1995: 100–101). **Midsummer Night** *A Midsummer Night's Dream*
        (1596), Shakespeare's comedy of thwarted lovers and fairy royalty.

p.79   *Dawn.* **Ben Jonson** see *If Ben Jonson Were Back* (p.136).

p.80   *The Poet Walking.* **Eastway** Eastgate Street, one of Gloucester's four
        principal roads. **Kineburgh's Cottage** see *Thoughts of New England*
        (p.129).

p.81   *The Comparison.* see *The Touchstone (Watching Malvern)* (p.129).
        Worcestershire to Herefordshire beacon two of the highest peaks
        on the Malvern Hills and popular vantage points for visitors.

p.81   *Strange Hells.* **'Après la guerre fini'** A bawdy trench song, sung to the
        tune of 'The Bridges of Paris', anticiapting how 'Soldat Anglais parti'
        once the war is over. **12 inch —6 inch and 18 pounders** sizes of high
        explosive shell and heavy artillery.

p.82 *Crickley Morning.* **screed** an unduly long harangue, from the Middle English. **Chaucer** Gurney described Geoffrey Chaucer (*circa* 1343–1400), the author of *Troilus and Criseyde* and *The Canterbury Tales*, as '(at his best) most human, most tender' (Thornton 1991: 509). **Milton** John Milton (1608–74), the English poet best known for *Comus* (1634), *Lycidas* (1673) and *Paradise Lost* (1667). Gurney regarded him as 'one of the great men not worth crossing the street to see' (Thornton 1991: 40).

p.83 *That Centre of Old.* **strafe** see *Laventie* (p.128).

p.84 *Incredible Thing.* **the mutineers** see 'Germanicus' in *Tobacco* (p.126). **Scyllas** Scylla was a mythical sea monster who dwelt on the island of Scylla opposite Charybdis, and was a terror to ships and sailors. Whenever a ship passed, each of her six heads would seize one of the crew. **Titus** Titus Flavius Vespasianus, the Roman general and statesman who was the son of Vespasian and the lover of Berenice. He was Emperor of Rome between AD 79–81. **Galba** Servius Sulpicius Galba, the Roman soldier and statesman who served briefly as emperor between AD 68 and 69 before being murdered by mutinous troops.

p.85 *Up Horsepools.* **Ford** John Ford (*circa* 1586–1640), the dramatist. Little is known about his life but he is most famous for *'Tis Pity She's a Whore* (1631). **Gloriana's great writers** Gloriana was one of the names used by Elizabethan poets to refer to Elizabeth I. **the Mermaid print** Havelock Ellis's edition of Ford's plays, containing *The Lover's Melancholy*, *'Tis Pity She's a Whore*, *The Broken Heart*, *Love's Sacrifice* and *Perkin Warbeck*, was published as part of the Mermaid series in 1888. **Morley** Professor Henry Morley (1838–1923) was a prolific editor, literary historian and compiler of anthologies of English literature. In 'Elizabethans', Gurney talks of paying 'half a crown' for 'Morley' (Thornton & Walter 1995: 80), and extracts from most of the playwrights he mentions can be found in the *English Plays* volume of Morley's 214 volume *Cassell's National Library of English Literature* series (1886–90). **Marston** John Marston (*circa* 1575–1634), the dramatist perhaps best known for *The Malcontent* (1604). **Greene** see *Cyril Tourneur* (p.131). **Shirley** James Shirley (1596–1666), the dramatist and author of some forty comedies, tragedies and masques, including *The Traitor* (1631) and *The Lady of Pleasure* (1635).

p.85 *Crickley.* **Titans** in Greek mythology, twelve pre-Olypian gods who were the sons of Uranus and Ge. **conies** an archaic or dialect term for rabbits. **kites** birds of prey. **Virgil** Publius Vergilius Maro (70–19 BC), the Roman poet born in Mantua. His twelve-book epic, *The Aeneid*, tells the story of the wanderings and vicissitudes of Aeneas and his crew after the Fall of Troy. Gurney described *The Aenieid* as 'a halting business' but regarded Virgil as 'a marvellous verse writer' (Thornton 1991: 516).

Catullus Gaius Valerius Catullus (*circa* 84–54 BC), the Roman poet and epigrammatist best known for his love poems to Lesbia. **She of Asia** possibly an allusion to Cleopatra. **of Mantuan earth** see 'Virgil' above. **Companion Lamps** an extension of the metaphor used in 'The Companions' (Kavanagh 1982: 59), where Gurney imagines the stars as his comrades whilst on a night-time journey. **Constantine** Flavius Valerius Constatinus (AD 306–37), the Roman statesman known as 'Constantine the Great'. He reigned as emperor from AD 323 until his death. **Beethoven** see *Thoughts on Beethoven* (p.137).

p.88   *The Fatigue Party.* **Fatigue** a soldier's non-military duties, such as digging, wire-mending or food preparation. **Verey lights** see *Tobacco* (p.126). **Leviathan** the Hebrew name for a monster of the waters, alluded to in Job 41:1, Psalms 104: 25–26 and Isaiah 27:1. **Samson** Judges 13:24 to 16:31 tells the story of the Nazirite Samson, whose legendary strength was taken away from him when Delilah cut his hair and blinded him. **duckboards** see *First Time In* (p.141). **The friend who drew my heart out to the heart of Beethoven** see *Thoughts of Beethoven* (p.137).

p.88   *Bacon of Mornings.* **the other (Shakespeare) Bacon** an allusion to the belief that Francis Bacon (1561–1626), the philosopher and statesman whose works include *The Advancement of Learning* (1605) and *Novum Organum* (1620), was the real author of Shakespeare's plays. **the Slaughters** Upper Slaughter is one of only forty 'Thankful Villages' in Britain, so-called because they lack a memorial to the local dead of the Great War. **Chapman** George Chapman (*circa* 1599–1634), the poet and playwright chiefly known for his translations of Homer's *Iliad* (1611) and *Odyssey* (1614–15). **Ben Jonson** see *If Ben Jonson Were Back* (p.136).

p.90   *Merville.* **Gloucester's tall / Tower** Gloucester Cathedral. **strawn** dialect for 'strewn'.

p.90   *New Year's Eve.* See *Crucifix Corner* (p.134). **limbers** the detachable front part of a gun carriage. **dugout** the military term for a roofed shelter in the trenches, also ironically known as a 'funk-hole'. **screed** see *Crickley Morning* (p.139). **Sir Walter** see *Crucifix Corner* (p.134). **Burns** Robert Burns (1759–96), the Scottish poet baptised and educated in Ayr who is perhaps best known today for 'Auld Lang Syne' and 'My luve's like a red, red rose'. **Perthshire** see 'Sir Walter' in *Crucifix Corner* (p.134). **Ayrshire** see 'Burns' above. **Forth** see *If Ben Jonson Were Back* (p.136). *Spirit of Man* The Spirit of Man (1916), the anthology assembled by the poet Robert Bridges (1844–1930). Writing to Mrs Voynich in August 1916, Gurney judged it to be 'very far below what it might be . . . About one third of the book is worth having, some of it foolish merely' (Thornton 1991: 140). **Borrow** see *Deerhurst*

Church (p.138). **'A Hundred Pipers'** see *Crucifix Corner* (p.134).

p.92   *Billet.* **billet** the military term for a place of rest assigned to soldiers. **Brewery** probably the Frome Brewery mentioned in 'Stroud' in *The book of Five makings*: 'Dost remember what equal wages | They paid at Frome Brewery 'fore it went to bankruptcy' (Thornton & Walter 1995: 131). **'Traveller's Rest'** a public house in Stroud. **estaminets** see *Riez Bailleul* (p.134). **café-au-lait** see *Laventie* (p.128). **dixie-lid** see *Riez Bailleul Also* (p.134).

p.93   *Rouen.* **Yea and Nay** an allusion to the rigid disciplinary methods by which the British Army ensured that its troops appreciated the importance of drill. **Balzac** Honoré de Balzac (1799–1850), the French novelist whose *Le Curé de Tours* (1832) is a study of clerical life in Tours. **Nelson** Horatio, 1st Viscount Nelson (1758–1805), the English admiral famous for his victory over the French at the Battle of Trafalgar. **Gallipoli** the site in the Dardanelles where determined Turkish resistance succesfully repelled a British and Anzac invasion between April 1915 and January 1916.

p.93   *Glimmering Dusk.* **Marston** see *Up Horsepools* (p.139). **Cyril Tourneur** see *Cyril Tourneur* (p.131).

p.94   *Loam Lies Heavy.* **frore** an archaism meaning 'frozen' or 'frosty'. **Orion** see *When The Sun Leaps Tremendous* (p.131). **Sirius** see *Half Dead* (p.128). **Argo** see *Half Dead* (p.128).

p.95   *Crucifix Corner.* See *Crucifix Corner* (p.134) and *New Year's Eve* (p.140).

p.96   *The Abbey.* See 'Peter's Abbey' in *Thoughts of New England* (p.129). **grew** a footnote on the Vaughan Williams typescript notes that this is 'A Scottish word'; the Oxford English Dictionary defines it as Scots dialect for 'Greek'.

p.96   *I Saw England (July Night).* **Will Squele** the 'Cotswold man' mentioned in Act II, Scene 2 of Shakespeare's *Henry IV, Part 2* (1600). **Twelfth Night** Shakespeare's Illyrian comedy, first published in the Quarto of 1623. Gurney seems to associate the play with England because of allusions to 'the bed of Ware' in Act III, Scene 2 and the Elephant and Castle in Act III, Scene 3. **Edward Thomas** see *Glory — and Quiet Glory* (p.126). **Borrow** see *Deerhurst Church* (p.138). **Hardy** see *Praise of Tobacco* (p.128). **Sussex tales out of Roman heights callen** see 'where Kipling loved and ranged' in *Thoughts of New England* (p.130).

p.97   *First Time In.* The 2/5th Gloucesters' first experience of trench warfare was on 29 May 1916, when they relieved the 15th Royal Welch Fusiliers (London Welsh) the battalion to which the poet and artist David Jones belonged in the Front Line opposite Riez Bailleul. Gurney and Basil Cridlan shared a dug-out with 'four of the nicest young men you could meet, possibly. They knew folksong. And one of them sang 'David of the White Rock' and 'A Slumber Song', both of which Somervell has arranged, and both beauties . . . a most amazing evening' (Thornton 1991: 89). **billet** see *Billet* (p.141). **duckboard** a narrow slatted path of wood laid over wet and muddy ground. **Verey lights** see *Tobacco* (p.126). **Reserve Line** see 'the Line' in *Laventie* (p.128). **tin hat** a soldiers' nickname for the basin-shaped shrapnel helmets first issued to the BEF in August 1915. **on Rest** see 'the Line' in *Laventie* (p.128). **the Plain** Salisbury Plain, where the 2/5th Gloucesters were stationed between February and May 1916. *Cranford* the novel depicting gentility in a quiet Cheshire village by Elizabeth Gaskell (1810–65), first published in book form in 1853. **Trollope** Anthony Trollope (1815–82), the English novelist most famous for his 'Chronicles of Barset' novels of manners, such as *The Warden* (1855) and *Framley Parsonage* (1861). **Minnie-werfers** see *Tobacco* (p.126). **dugouts** see *New Year's Eve* (p.140). **the 'Slumber Song'** probably the traditional Welsh lullaby 'All Through the Night', which talks of how 'Soft the drowsy hours are creeping | Hill and vale in slumber sleeping'. **the soft Chant** Gurney may have in mind one of the mildly obscene versions of the Salvation Army hymn 'Wash Me in the Water' popular during the war or perhaps 'Big Willie's Luvly Daughter', a variant of 'Where are the Boys of the Village Tonight' favoured by the Welch Fusiliers which suggested that 'the object of the British Expedition into France was to enjoy the charms of the Emperor's daughter' (Jones 1937: 213). **'David of the White Rock'** also known by its Welsh title *Dafydd y Garreg Wen*, this folksong was highly popular amongst the Welch Fusiliers (Jones 1937: 197). **the Golden Age** the idyllic mythological era when Kronos ruled and and men were happy, innocent and at their most creative. **'Widdicombe Fair'** see *At The Inn* (p.132). **Fritz** the nickname given to the Germans by the British army during the First World War. **strafed** see *Laventie* (p.128).

p.99   *The Unvisited Church*. Probably St Mary's in Painswick. Located beside a road and overlooked by Painswick Beacon, it dates largely from the Middle Ages but its early seventeenth-century spire had to be renovated in 1883 after being struck by lightning. **though the so-wanted | Beauty was not found truth was kept** Gurney's reading of John Keats' famous truism that 'Beauty is truth, Truth beauty' in his 'Ode on a Grecian Urn'.

p.100   *Poem For End*. **Crucifix Corner** see *Crucifix Corner* (p.134). **the dead Master** presumably Ben Jonson, given the frequency with which he is mentioned in *Rewards of Wonder*.

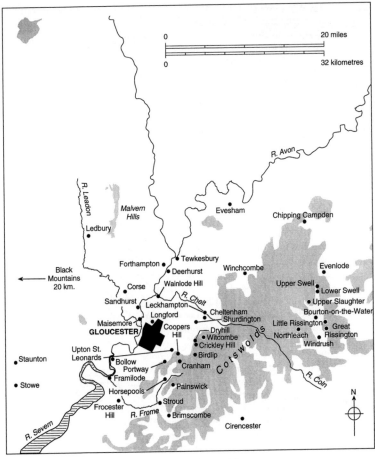

Gurney's Cotswolds

Gurney's France

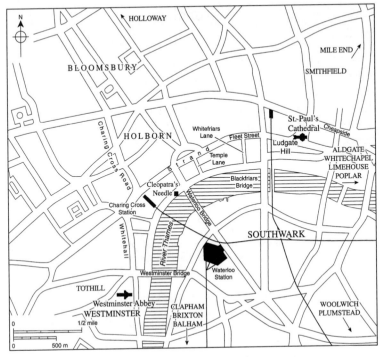

Gurney's London

Chronology

This Chronology presents a detailed account of Gurney's life and artistic activities, stressing in particular the circumstances surrounding the creation, revision and reproduction of *Rewards of Wonder*. It draws on a variety of unpublished and published sources, such as Gurney's own letters and manuscripts, his medical records, correspondence between his friends and the account books kept by Marion Scott after Gurney's committal in 1922.

1890 28 August	Ivor Bertie Gurney born at 3 Queen Street, Gloucester, the second child of David Gurney, a tailor, and Florence Lugg. Alfred Hunter Cheesman, the curate at All Saints' Church, acts as godfather at his christening. The family move to 19 Barton Street, house and shop, shortly after Gurney's birth.
1894	Gurney's younger brother, Ronald, is born.
1896	Gurney starts attending the National School and All Saints' Sunday School. The Gurney family purchase their first piano.
1899	Gurney joins the choir of All Saints' Church.
1900	Gurney wins a place in Gloucester Cathedral Choir and starts attending the King's School, where he learns the organ. His younger sister, Dorothy, is born.
1904	Gurney sings with Madame Albani at the Three Choirs Festival. He begins to write music.
1905	Gurney begins his close association with Canon Cheesman and Margaret and Emily Hunt, all of whom encourage his creative talents.
1906	Gurney leaves the Cathedral Choir and the King's School to become an articled pupil of Dr. Herbert Brewer, the organist

of Gloucester Cathedral. He makes friends with Herbert Howells, a fellow pupil of Brewer's, F. W. Harvey and John Wilton Haines. He works temporarily as an organist at Whitminster, Hempsted and the Mariners' Church in Gloucester's Docklands.

| 1907 | Gurney passes the matriculation examination for Durham University. |

1907 — Gurney passes the matriculation examination for Durham University.

1910 — Gurney and Howells attend the première of Vaughan Williams' *Fantasia on a Theme by Thomas Tallis* in Gloucester.

1911 — Gurney wins an open scholarship for composition at the Royal College of Music of £40 per annum, with Cheesman providing another £40. He takes digs in Fulham. He is taught composition by Charles Villiers Stanford and makes friends with Marion M. Scott and Ethel Voynich.

1912 — Howells wins a composition scholarship to the Royal College of Music. He and Gurney make friends with another new student, Arthur Benjamin.

1913 — Gurney begins to write poetry seriously.
May — He is diagnosed as suffering from dyspepsia and 'neurasthenia' by Dr. Harper and returns to Gloucestershire to recuperate.
Winter — He writes his settings of five Elizabethan lyrics – what he calls 'The Elizas'.

1914
August — Gurney volunteers for military service but is rejected because of his defective eyesight.
October — He takes the post of organist at Christ Church, High Wycombe, where he makes the acquaintance of the Chapman family. He falls in love with Kitty Chapman and asks for permission to marry her. It is refused.

1915
9 February — Gurney volunteers again and is drafted into the 5th Gloucester Reserve Battalion, the '2/5th Glosters', as Private no. 3895. He spends the rest of the year in training at Northampton, Chelmsford and Epping.

August	He begins to send Marion Scott his poems and rediscovers the poetry of Walt Whitman, writing to Ethel Voynich that 'he has taken me like a flood'.
December	'Afterwards' and 'To the Poet Before Battle' are published in *The Royal College of Music Magazine*.

1916

February	The 2/5th Glosters move to Tidworth and then on to Park House Camp on Salisbury Plain.
25 May	They arrive in Le Havre and are then sent into trenches at Riez Bailleul.
8 June	They move on to Laventie.
15 June	They relieve the 2nd/1st Bucks in the Fauquissart-Laventie sector. They are billeted at La Gorgue.
July	'To Certain Comrades' is published in *The Royal College of Music Magazine*.
19 July	They are placed in reserve for the attack on Aubers Ridge and 'on Rest' at Richebourg, Neuve-Chappelle, Robecq and Gonnehem.
28 August	Gurney is admitted to a Casualty Clearing Station to have his teeth treated.
27 October	The Battalion moves south to Albert and the Somme sector.
December	Gurney is sent to a Rest Station with 'a cold in the stomach' and then takes a temporary job with the water carts in the Sanitary Section at 61st Divisional Headquarters.

1917

7 January	Gurney returns to normal duties.
15 February	The 2/5th Glosters are moved to the Ablaincourt sector.
18 March	They follow the German withdrawal to Caulaincourt and then on to Vermand.
7 April	Gurney is wounded on Good Friday in the upper arm and sent to hospital at the 55th Infantry Base Depot, Rouen. He is given a new Army Number, 241281.
18 May	He is back with the Battalion, which moves to the Arras Front.
23 June	The 2/5th Glosters are 'on Rest' at Buire-au-Bois. Gurney becomes his platoon's crack shot.
July	'Song of Pain and Beauty' is published in *The Royal College of Music Magazine*.
14 July	Sidgwick & Jackson agree to publish Gurney's poems.
15 July	Gurney transfers to the 184 Machine Gun Company at Vaux.
31 July	The Battalion moves on to Buysscheure in reserve for the

	battle of Passchendaele.
10 September	Gurney is gassed at St. Julien.
25 September	He arrives at the Edinburgh War Hospital, Bangour, where he meets and falls in love with Annie Nelson Drummond, a V.A.D. nurse. Their relationship does not last.
November	'Strange Service', 'Afterwards', 'To Certain Comrades' and 'To the Poet Before Battle' are published in E. B. Osborn's anthology *The Muse in Arms*. *Severn & Somme* is published. Gurney is transferred to Seaton Delaval for a signalling course.

1918

12 February	Gurney is granted leave to visit his sick father.
25 February	He is examined for the effects of gas and admitted to Newcastle General Hospital.
March	He is moved to Brancepeth Castle, a convalescent depot.
28 March	He writes to Marion Scott telling her that he has spoken to 'the spirit of Beethoven', clearly a sign of some kind of nervous breakdown.
April	'Ypres' and 'After Music' are published in *The Royal College of Music Magazine*.
22 April	He returns to Newcastle General Hospital and is then moved on to Seaton Delaval.
8 May	He is sent to Lord Derby's War Hospital, Warrington. Hospitals in the area are using 'Faradisation' – controlled electrical charges – as a treatment for shell-shock, though there is no evidence of its use on Gurney.
June	'The Immortal Hour' is published in *The Westminster Gazette*.
19 June	He sends a suicide note to Marion Scott and tells his superiors that he hears voices and wishes to be sent to an asylum.
4 July	He is sent to Middlesex War Hospital in St. Albans.
4 October	He is discharged from the army with a pension of 12 shillings a week. He is not granted a full pension because his condition is 'aggravated but not caused by' the war. He returns to 19 Barton Street, Gloucester.
October	He is working in a munitions factory and worrying his friends and family with his erratic behaviour. He makes several attempts to go to sea. The Chapman family offer to adopt him, but his own family do not allow this.
11 November	He finishes work at the munitions factory.
7 December	'The Battalion is Now "On Rest"' is published in *The Spectator*.
Christmas	He goes to stay with Ethel Voynich in Cornwall.

1919

January	Gurney returns to the Royal College of Music, where Ralph Vaughan Williams is his composition teacher. He moves into digs in West Kensington. *Severn & Somme* is reprinted.
11 January	'In a Ward' is published in *The Spectator*. 'The Day of Victory' is published in *The Gloucester Journal*.
22 February	'The Volunteer' is published in *The Spectator*.
25 February	Gurney returns to 19 Barton Street to correct the proofs of *War's Embers*, his second volume for Sidgwick & Jackson. He tells Marion Scott: 'Book three you see is in the making!'
3 March	Margaret Hunt dies.
22 April	He is working at Dryhill Farm, Shurdington.
May	He is living in St. John's Wood, London. *War's Embers* is published.
10 May	His father, David Gurney, dies.
August	He submits poems to *The Century*, *The Athenæum*, *Harper's Magazine*, *The New Witness* and *The Spectator*, none of which are accepted. He goes on a walking tour of the Black Mountains with John Haines and moves to High Wycombe on his return.
September	He takes a post as organist at Christ Church, High Wycombe.
October	He is suffering from 'nerves and an inability to think or write at all clearly', yet is now moving in London literary circles.
8 November	He and F. W. Harvey visit John Masefield at Boar's Hill, Oxford.

1920

Late February	Gurney walks from High Wycombe to Dryhill Farm via Oxford.
March	'The Twa Corbies' is published in *Music and Letters*.
May	He tries to set up home in a cottage at Cold Slad, Dryhill.
July	'The Hooligan' and 'April 20th 1919' are published in *The Royal College of Music Magazine*. Stainer & Bell publish 'Captain Stratton's Fancy'. Winthrop Rogers publish 'Orpheus', 'Sleep', 'Tears', 'Spring' and 'Under the Greenwood Tree' – 'The Elizas'. Boosey & Co. publish 'Carol of the Skiddaw Yowes'.
October	Gurney is living in lodgings in Earls Court, London. 'Equal Mistress' and 'The Crocus Ring' are published in *Music and Letters*.
6 November	He receives a Government Grant of £120 a year, backdated to 25 September. He meets Edmund Blunden and Wilfrid Gibson for the first time.

18 December	'Desire in Spring' is published in *The Chapbook*.
1921	Chappell & Co. publish 'West Sussex Drinking Song'. Boosey & Co. publish 'I will go with my father a-ploughing'.
12 February	'Fine Rain' is published in *The Nation*.
March	Boosey & Co. publish 'Since thou, O fondest and truest'.
April	Gurney is living with his aunt at 1 Westfield Terrace, Longford, Gloucester. He tries unsuccessfully to get his poems included in Edward Marsh's anthology *Georgian Poetry 1920–1922* and looks for and eventually finds work on a farm.
May	'Song of Pain and Beauty' and 'To the Poet Before Battle' are reprinted in J. C. Squire's anthology, *Selections from Modern Poets*.
June–July	He is living at the Five Alls, Stokenchurch, near High Wycombe.
Late July	He formally leaves the Royal College of Music and returns to his aunt's house in Longford.
August	He works in a cold storage depot in Southwark for a fortnight and then returns to Longford, finding employment on a farm.
20 August	'Western Sky' is published in *The Nation and Athenæum*.
September	Winthrop Rogers publish 'The Bonnie Earl of Murray' and 'The County Mayo'. Gurney is probably using the black and green manuscript notebooks by this time.
October	Winthrop Rogers publish the *Five Preludes for Piano*.
December	He obtains a post playing the piano at a cinema in Bude but is retained for only a week.
1922	Stainer & Bell publish 'Edward, Edward'. Boosey & Co. publish 'Come, O come my Life's delight'.
January	Gurney is living in Walham Green, London, and probably using the pink marbled manuscript notebook by this time.
7 January	'This City' is published in *The Gloucester Journal*.
Mid January	Gurney moves to Plumstead, London, and finds a job playing the piano in a cinema there. He is retained only for a fortnight.
February	He returns to his aunt's house in Longford and finds work on a farm.
April	Dorothy Gurney types out selections from his poems out for him.
15 April	'On a Two Hundredth Birthday' is published in *The Gloucester Journal*.
May	He looks for a job in the Civil Service and submits a volume of

	'80 poems or so' to Sidgwick & Jackson, who return it and advise him to reduce and revise its contents.
10 June	'Tewkesbury' is published in *The Gloucester Journal*. Gurney resubmits his poems to Sidgwick & Jackson but they are rejected again.
July	His essay, 'The Springs of Music', is published in *The Musical Quarterly*. He is now writing 'War poems. (rather bad.)'.
3 July	He begins work at the Gloucester Tax Office but loses his post after twelve weeks.
September	He moves in uninvited with his brother Ronald and his wife at 52 Worcester Street, Gloucester. His behaviour becomes very disturbed and he makes a number of suicide attempts.
Late September	He goes to a Convalescent Home near Bristol but his condition does not improve.
28 September	He is certified insane by Dr. Soutar and Dr. Terry and is admitted to Barnwood House, a private asylum near Gloucester.
October	'Encounters' and 'The March Past' are published in *The London Mercury*.
21 October	Gurney escapes but is recaptured after a few hours.
8 November	He escapes again but is recaptured at a police station.
21 December	He is transferred to the City of London Mental Hospital at Dartford – known as 'Stone House' or 'Dr. Steen's' – and comes under the care of Dr. Robinson, the Second Assistant Medical Officer.
1923	Stainer & Bell publish the song cycle *Ludlow and Teme* as part of the Carnegie Collection of British Music and the *Five Western Watercolours*.
January	'Sights' is published in *The London Mercury*.
6 January	Gurney escapes whilst walking in the hospital grounds and travels to London. He visits J. C. Squire and Ralph Vaughan Williams, who informs the authorities. He is recaptured and returned to Dartford via Hounslow Infirmary.
February	His physical condition improves but his mental condition remains the same.
31 March	'The Road' is published in *The Spectator*.
May	'Advice' is published in *The London Mercury*. Gurney is correcting the typescripts of the green and pink marbled manuscript notebooks and planning 'a thick book of verse'.
June	Ronald Gurney sends his brother's manuscripts to Marion Scott. John Haines also begins to gather material.

August	Gurney's condition is treated with 'Malarial injections', which have no effect on his mental state.
Christmas	He entertains his fellow-patients with his piano-playing during the festivities.

1924

January	'Thoughts of New England', 'New Year's Eve', 'Old Tale', 'The Cloud', 'Smudgy Dawn', 'Tobacco' and 'Brimscombe' are published in *The London Mercury*. Gurney receives seven visits from Dr. Cyriax, an osteopath, for treatment for pains in his neck and head.
March	He refuses to get up from his bed in the veranda. His mental condition worsens.
July	His contribution to 'Charles Villiers Stanford. By Some of His Pupils' is published in *Music and Letters*. Miss Mollie Hart is paid £1.5s for typing out the first version of *Rewards of Wonder*.
August	He sends out a number of appeals listing seven new books of poems and who they have apparently been sent to. *Roman gone East* has gone to Arthur Benjamin, *Fatigues and Magnificences* has been sent to Basil Cridlan and Sir George Macmillan has apparently received a copy of *Rewards of Wonder*.
October	He corrects *Rewards of Wonder* to produce the second version of it.
November	The song *Lights Out* is published in *The London Mercury*. 'Thoughts of New England', 'Smudgy Dawn' and 'Dawn' are reprinted in J. C. Squire's anthology, *Second Selections from Modern Poets*. Gurney produces a number of revisions of these poems.
December	He is writing new poems and song settings. He receives 'French books'.

1925

	'Sleep' is reprinted in *A Miscellany of Artistic Songs*. 'I will go with my father a-ploughing' and 'Carol of the Skiddaw Yowes' are reprinted in *50 Modern English Songs*.
January	Gurney produces a prolific amount of songs and poems, including a collection for Annie Nelson Drummond called *To Hawthornden*.
February	He writes *The book of Five makings* and 'corrects' the green manuscript notebook. He also writes four song settings.
March	He writes seven song settings, including three of French poems, and many single poems. He also produces six new

collections of verse – *Memories of Honour*, *Poems to the States*, *Six Poems of the North American States*, *Poems in Praise of Poets*, *The Book of Lives and Accusations* and *Poems of Gloucesters, Gloucester and of Virginia*. Dr. Robinson is replaced by Dr. Randolph Davis, a Canadian with whom Gurney forms a rapport. Gerald Finzi approaches Marion Scott about the publication of Gurney's songs.

27 March | Arthur Benjamin performs two of Gurney's songs at a concert at Stone House.

April | 'Schubert' is published in *Music and Letters*. He writes many single poems and four song settings, including one to his own words called 'Song of the Canadian Soldiers'.

May | Dr. Davis is replaced by Dr. Anderson.

June | Gurney writes *Pictures and Memories* and many single poems. He also produces seven songs.

July | Stainer & Bell publish 'Sowing'. Gurney writes five songs and one choral setting.

August | His condition shows signs of slight improvement.

September | He writes eight song settings and some instrumental music.

November | Gurney is using the blue 'Marspen' exercise books. Marion Scott and Ralph Vaughan Williams make plans to transfer Gurney to Dr. Davis' care as a private patient.

December | The plan of handing Gurney over to Dr. Davis is suddenly abandoned.

1926 | Stainer & Bell publish the song cycle *Lights Out*.

January | Dr. Hart, a Harley Street psychiatrist, is consulted about Gurney's condition.

April | The song cycle *The Western Playland (and of sorrow)* is published as part of the Carnegie Collection of British Music. Gurney completes *Best poems*, using material from the 'Marspen' notebooks. He is taken by Marion Scott to the Old Vic and later writes a play called *The Tewkesbury Trial*.

September | He produces a prolific amount of new poems but his mental condition worsens.

November | His mental condition further deteriorates and he becomes agitated, stating that he 'should be allowed to die'. He refuses to be examined and asserts that an inspection of the floor and ceiling to find the machines torturing him would be more effective.

December | He becomes severely deluded and believes himself to be Shakespeare, Hilaire Belloc, Beethoven and Haydn, amongst others.

1927 February	Stainer & Bell publish 'Star Talk'. Gurney is treated by Mr. Lidderdale, a Christian Science practitioner, on the advice of Adeline Vaughan Williams.
March April	He is provided with a table to work at in the hospital gardens. 'Beethoven I wronged thee undernoting thus' is published in *Music and Letters*. He is mentally 'very confused' and his treatment with Mr. Lidderdale is terminated.
May June	He revises and 'corrects' poems by Walt Whitman. He becomes hostile to hospital staff and fellow-patients and his physical condition deteriorates.
1928	Oxford University Press publish 'Walking Song', 'Desire in Spring', 'The Fields are Full', 'Severn Meadows' and 'The Twa Corbies'. 'To the Poet Before Battle' is reprinted in Wallace Briggs' anthology *Great Poems of the English Language*. 'Song of Pain and Beauty' is reprinted in H. R. L. Sheppard and H. P. Marshall's anthology *Fiery Grains*.
February	Victor Gollancz expresses interest in publishing a collection of Gurney's poems. Marion Scott assembles a selection and copies them out. Gurney's eyes are examined by an oculist.
July	Miss Mollie Hart is paid 10s.9d for typing Marion Scott's selection of Gurney's poems.
1929 4 March	Gurney is taken to Gravesend and Rochester by Marion Scott. He wishes to buy a 'Phillips 1/- Atlas' but is unable to find one and Miss Scott buys him an edition of Shelley instead.
August 28 December	He claims to be the author of Shakespeare's plays. He visits the Old Vic with Marion Scott to see an afternoon performance of *A Midsummer Night's Dream*.
1930	'Song of Pain and Beauty' and 'To the Poet Before Battle' are reprinted in Frederick Brereton's *An Anthology of War Poems*. 'Song of Pain and Beauty' is also reprinted in W. H. Davies' anthology *Jewels of Song*.
1931	'Tobacco' and 'Encounters' are reprinted in *The Mercury Book of Verse*.
June	Gurney is 'very deluded & much persecuted by wireless speakers'. He hoards rubbish and becomes obsessed with 'underlining words in every book which he picks up'. However, he 'continues to write poetry'.

1932   Gurney receives a number of visits from Helen Thomas, the
                           widow of Edward Thomas.
November   'Tobacco' and 'Encounters' are reprinted in J. C. Squire's
                           anthology *Younger Poets of Today*.

1933
May   Gurney's physical and mental condition deteriorate further.
                           He becomes 'very abusive and forceful'.
December   'Darkness has Cheating Swiftness', 'Old Thought', 'Old
                           Dreams' and 'Towards Lillers' are published in *The London
                           Mercury*.

1934
January   'The Soaking', 'When March Blows', 'Robecq Again', 'Tea
                           Table', 'Early Spring Dawn' and 'When the Body Might
                           Free' are published in *The London Mercury*.
May   'Defiance', 'Late May' and 'The High Hills have a Bitterness'
                           are published in *The London Mercury*.
August   'Stars Sliding', 'Drachms and Scruples' and 'Possessions' are
                           published in *The London Mercury*. Gurney becomes apathetic
                           and his memory begins to fail. He now believes that 'Collins
                           the International' wrote Shakespeare's plays.

1935   Gerald Finzi and Marion Scott make plans for the publication
                           of a symposium on Gurney's work in *Music and Letters*. The
                           possibility of publishing his songs is also discussed.
May   Gurney receives treatment for his lumbago.

1937
February   Gerald Finzi and Marion Scott proceed with their plans for
                           the publication of Gurney's work. The *Music and Letters*
                           symposium begins to take shape.
April   Walter de la Mare agrees to write an introduction for an
                           edition of Gurney's poems.
June   Gerald Finzi types out poems of Gurney's which have
                           appeared in periodicals.
July   Gurney becomes 'much weaker' physically and mentally.
23 November   He is diagnosed as suffering from pleurisy and tuberculosis.
                           Marion Scott is urged to visit because he is in 'very poor
                           health'.
26 November   Proofs of the *Music and Letters* articles are sent to him, but he
                           is too ill to open them.

| 26 December | Gurney dies from bilateral pulmonary tuberculosis at 3.45 am. |
| 31 December | He is buried at Twigworth, Gloucestershire. Canon Cheesman takes the service. |

1938

| January | The symposium on Gurney's life and work is published in *Music and Letters*. *Ivor Gurney: Twenty Songs* is published by Oxford University Press in two volumes. |
| July | The BBC broadcast four recitals of Gurney's work. |

| 1939 | Plans for an edition of Gurney's unpublished poems are revived. John Haines agrees to make a selection and to have it copied. |

| 1940 | Two instrumental pieces by Gurney, *The Apple Orchard* and *Scherzo*, are published by Oxford University Press. |

| 1941 | Joyce Finzi, the wife of Gerald Finzi, discovers that John Haines has been too traumatised by the war to work on Gurney's manuscripts. She offers to type some material herself, but Marion Scott suggests that Miss E. Henry Bird, now her regular typist, should do it instead. |

| 1943 | Responding to Marion Scott's inactivity, Ralph Vaughan Williams has Gurney's poems copied by 'a very good typist in Dorking'. |

| 1948 | Edmund Blunden undertakes the production of a selection of Gurney's unpublished poems, using the Vaughan Williams typescripts as his primary source. |

| 1952 | *Ivor Gurney: A Third Volume of Ten Songs* is published by Oxford University Press. |

| 1953 | Marion Scott dies. |

| 1954 | Edmund Blunden's *Poems by Ivor Gurney: Principally selected from unpublished manuscripts* is published by Hutchinson. |

| 1956 | Gerald Finzi dies. |

| 1959 | *Ivor Gurney: A Fourth Volume of Ten Songs* is published by |

Oxford University Press. Ronald Gurney places his collection of his brother's manuscripts on permanent loan to Gloucester Library.

1973   Leonard Clark's *Poems of Ivor Gurney 1890–1937* is published by Chatto & Windus.

1978   Michael Hurd's *The Ordeal of Ivor Gurney* is published by Oxford University Press.

1982   P. J. Kavanagh's *Collected Poems of Ivor Gurney* is published by Oxford University Press.

1987   *Severn & Somme* and *War's Embers* are republished as a single volume by MidNAG & Carcanet.

1991   *Ivor Gurney: Collected Letters* is published by MidNAG & Carcanet.

1995   *Ivor Gurney: Best Poems and The Book of Five Makings* is published by MidNAG & Carcanet.

1997   *Ivor Gurney: 80 Poems or So* is published by MidNAG & Carcanet.

Texts Cited and Suggested Further Reading

Original Work by Gurney

Blunden, Edmund (ed.) 1954. *Poems by Ivor Gurney*. London: Hutchinson.

Clark, Leonard (ed.) 1973. *Poems of Ivor Gurney 1890–1937*. London: Chatto & Windus.

Hurd, Michael, Boden, Anthony & Wilson, Christian (eds) 1998. *Ivor Gurney: Eleven Songs for Medium Voice and Piano*. London: Thames Publishing.

Kavanagh, P.J. (ed.) 1982. *Collected Poems of Ivor Gurney*. London: Oxford University Press.

Thornton, R.K.R. (ed.) 1987. *Ivor Gurney: Severn & Somme and War's Embers*. Ashington & Manchester: MidNAG & Carcanet.

Thornton, R.K.R. (ed.) 1991. *Ivor Gurney: Collected Letters*. Ashington & Manchester: MidNAG & Carcanet.

Thornton, R.K.R. & Walter, George. (eds) 1995. *Ivor Gurney: Best Poems and The Book of Five Makings*. Ashington & Manchester: MidNAG & Carcanet.

Walter, George and Thornton, R.K.R. (eds) 1997. *Ivor Gurney: 80 Poems or So*. Ashington & Manchester: MidNAG & Carcanet.

Unpublished Material from the Gurney Archive

Gurney 5.12.2. manuscript letter from J.C. Squire to Marion Scott dated 19 October 1926.

Gurney 10.38. manuscript letter from Ivor Gurney to Marion Scott postmarked 18 October 1924.

Gurney 10.47. manuscript letter from Ivor Gurney to Marion Scott *circa* May 1923.

Gurney 11.1.2. cash book for Ivor Gurney's Midland Bank account for the period 1922 to 1938.

Gurney 42.6.13. typescript letter from John Haines to Marion Scott dated 4 February 1928.

Gurney 51. scrapbook of typed extracts from letters concerning the preservation and publication of Gurney's work from 1941 to 1959.

Gurney 52.11.132. undated manuscript letter from Gurney to Marion Scott.

Gurney 52.11.137. manuscript letter from Ivor Gurney to Sir Edward Marsh *circa* August 1924.

Gurney 52.11.141. manuscript letter from Ivor Gurney to Sir Robert Baden Powell *circa* August 1924.

Biographical and Critical Works

anon. 1937a. 'Death of Gloucester-Born "Schubert". Tragedy of Ivor Gurney's Unfulfilled Promise. War Suffering that Vitiated his Powers', *The Citizen*, 28 December 1937, 1.

anon. 1937b. 'Mr. Ivor Gurney: Poet and Musician', *The Times*, 28 December 1937, 14.

Barnes, A.F. 1930. *The Story of the 2/5th Battalion Gloucestershire Regiment 1914–1918*. Gloucester: Crypt House Press.

Black, E.L. (ed.) 1970. *1914–18 in Poetry*. London: London University Press.

Hurd, Michael. 1978. *The Ordeal of Ivor Gurney*. Oxford: Oxford University Press.

Jones, David. 1937. *In Parenthesis*. London: Faber and Faber.

Rattenbury, Arnold. 1999. 'How the sanity of poets can be edited away', *The London Review of Books*, Volume 21, Number 20, 14 October 1999, 15–19.

Scott, Marion M. 1938. 'Recollections of Ivor Gurney', *The Monthly Musical Record*, Volume 68, Number 794 (February 1938), 41–6.

Stephen, Martin (ed.) 1988. *Never Such Innocence: A New Anthology of Great War Verse*. London: Buchan & Enright.

Taylor, Martin 1987. 'Ivor Gurney: "Only the Wanderer"', *The Imperial War Museum Review*, Number 2, 98–105.

Works on Insanity

Claridge, Gordon. 1998. 'Creativity and Madness: Clues from Modern Psychiatric Diagnosis' in Andrew Steptoe (ed.), *Genius and the Mind: Studies of Creativity and Temperament*. Oxford: Oxford University Press, 227–52.

Claridge, Gordon, Pryor, Ruth & Watkins, Gwen. 1990. *Sounds From the Bell Jar: Ten Psychotic Authors*. Basingstoke: Macmillan.

Gottesman, Irving. 1991. *Schizophrenia Genesis: The Origins of Madness*. New York: W.H. Freeman and Company.

Howe, Gwen. 1991. *The Reality of Schizophrenia*. London: Faber and Faber.

Peterson, Dale (ed.) 1982. *A Mad People's History of Madness*. Pittsburgh: University of Pittsburgh Press.

Rhodes, Nicholas, Dowker, Ann & Claridge, Gordon. 1995. 'Subject Matter and Poetic Devices in Psychotics' Poetry', *British Journal of Medical Psychology*, Volume 68, Part 4, 287–372.

Rosenbaum, Bent & Sonne, Harly. 1986. *The Language of Psychosis*. New York and London: New York University Press.

Trethowan, W.H. 1981. 'Ivor Gurney's Mental Illness', *Music and Letters*, Volume LXII, Numbers 3–4, July/October 1981, 300–9.

Index of Titles and First Lines

A Country ignorant of its own songs   63
A million men before me had taken those steps   38
After the dread tales and red yarns of the Line   62
After War — Half War   44
Alas, for the singers, who might vamp chords   52
April is Happy   35
April is happy now her sowing's done   35
As any blue thing can be the ford was blue   45
As any blue thing can be the ford was good   36
At the Inn   52
Aveluy and New Year's Eve, and the time as tender   90

Bacon of Mornings   88
Beethoven I wronged thee undernoting thus   72
Billet   92
Blighty   67
Brimscombe   99
Buysscheure   79
By Severn   31

Canadians   43
Clouds Die Out In June   66
Clouds die out in June where the sun drops   66
Cotswold   63
Cotswold Edge shines out at morning in gold   63
Cotswold Slopes   50
Crickley   85
Crickley makes clouds to gather there   85
Crickley Morning   82
Crucifix Corner   60
Crucifix Corner   95
Cyril Tourneur   47
Cyril Tourneur, avid of name and fame   47

Darkness Has Cheating Swiftness   37
Darkness has cheating swiftness   37
Dawn   79
Dawn brings lovely playthings to the mind   77
Dawn came not surprising but later widened   28

Dawn comes queerly in late May   78
Deerhurst Church   76
Disappointment comes to all men, if so the church   99

Early Spring Dawn   62

Fire and water makes a home's centre   70
First March   48
First Time In   62
First Time In   97
For two grains of wheat grown on Waltheof's field   67
Ford that I could not read, but spent miles of road on   85
France has Victory, England yet firm shall stay   92
Friendly Are Meadows   94
Friendly are meadows when the sun's gone down in   94
From the racked substance of the earth comes the plant and   47

Georgian with a stairway up to the roof   32
Gifts and Courtesy   54
Glimmering Dusk   93
Glimmering dusk above the moist plough and the   93
Glory — and Quiet Glory   24
Gloucester streets walking in Autumn twilight   39
Great Jonson praised tobacco as was fit   33

Half Dead   25
Half Dead   61
Half dead with sheer tiredness, wakened quick at night   25
Half dead with tiredness, wakened quick at night   61

I am not jealous of any town for Gloucester   93
I Saw England (July Night)   96
I saw people   80
If Ben Jonson he were back what strong things then   70
If Ben Jonson Were Back   70
If England, her spirit lives anywhere   31
If I could know the quarry where these stones grew   96
If one's heart is broken twenty times a day   72
Incredible Thing   84
Is it only Cotswold that holds the glamour   83
It seemed that it were well to kiss first earth   67
It was agreed that Carthage should be rased   36
It was first marching, hardly had we settled yet   48

June's Meadows   74

Kilns   55

La Gorgues   64
Late May   78
Laventie   34
Laventie Dawn   28
Laventie Front   45
Laventie Ridge   68
Leckhampton Elbow   28
Loam Lies Heavy   94
Loam lies heavy on the lightless flesh   94
Long shines the thin light of the day to north-east   62
Lovely Playthings   77
Lying flat on my belly shivering in clutch-frost   51

Man takes the heaven of glories for his own   24
Many times I have seen windmills, or grassy slopes   79
Memory   83
Merville   90
Morning struck the first steel of cloud light   82
Mostly I remember high days and afterglows   54

Near Vermand   51
New Year's Eve   90
Northleach   65
Northleach, that jewel, white stone and green foliage   65
Not a thing to see, pitch black-misty rainy night   88

O, but the racked clear tired strained frames we had!   92
October   23
Of Bricks and Brick Pits   49
Of Cruelty   47
Of the kilns that saw the Siege, that saved England   49
Of Trees Over There   53
Old Tale   72
One could not see or think, the heat overcame one   52
One got peace of heart at last, the dark march over   44
One lucky hour in middle of my tiredness   99
One would remember still   34
One would remember still   45
Only at certain times the tourists go there   30

Poem For End   100
Poets   74
Possessions   92
Praise of Tobacco   33
Prelude (12/8 Time)   76

Queen of Cotswold   30

Riez Bailleul   57
Riez Bailleul Also   58
Riez Bailleul in blue tea-time   57
Roads — Those Roads   75
Roads are sometimes the true symbolical   75
Robecq   51
Robecq — A Memory   91
Robecq that's swept away now, so men tell   91
Robecq, that's all swept away now, so men tell   51
Roman, and the War Poet   55
Rouen   93

Severn has kilns set all along her banks   55
Severn Meadows   44
She was a village   96
Sheer Falls of Green Slope   69
Sheer falls of green slope against setting sun   69
Shepherd's warning, and all too gay forerunning   83
Small Chubby Dams   73
Small chubby dams banked in the water   73
Smudgy Dawn   59
Smudgy dawn scarfed with military colours   59
So the last poem is laid flat in its place   100
Soft veils of dusk wrapping Severn meadows   44
Songs Come To The Mind   78
Songs come to the mind   78
Strange Hells   81
Student Days   38
Swathes laid breaker like in long shore waves   74

Tewkesbury   71
Tewkesbury, that square thing, name of stone and battle   71
That Centre of Old   83
The Abbey   96
The Bargain   36

The Bargain   67
The Captain addressed us. After glow grew deeper   97
The Cloud   52
The Comparison   81
The Essential Things   70
The Fatigue Party   88
The Ford   36
The Ford   38
The Ford   45
The gaiety of colours   76
The lantern made a green broad radiance   23
The Lantern–Shine   23
The long night, the short sleep, and La Gorgues to wander   64
The low ridge of Laventie   68
The mutineers, true Romans that once were Scyllas   84
The Poet Walking   80
The rain has come, and the earth must be very glad   89
The sick mind grows whole in October gales   23
The Soaking   89
The Song   63
The Tax Office   32
The Touchstone (Watching Malvern)   39
The unclean hells and the different Hell's terrors   61
The Unvisited Church   99
The whitest thing in life save Gloucester's tall   90
There's dusk here; West hedgerows show thin   58
There are strange Hells within the minds War made   81
There is a scorn of mankind in the short grassed   55
There is something wrong there, with that the gracefullest   76
There was a water dump there and regimental   60
There was a water dump there, and regimental   95
There were Ypres trees as bad as cabbage stumps   53
Thoughts of New England   39
Thoughts on Beethoven   72
To see the dawn soak darkness, look out now   79
To the West Country dawn comes with crystal breath   88
Tobacco   26
Tobacco   29
Today   61

Up Horsepools   85

We marched, and saw a Company of Canadians   43

What I Will Pay   58
What I will pay to my God is that I will not sleep between sheets   58
What Malvern is the day is, and its touchstone   39
What Malvern is the day is, and its touchstone   81
When a cloud is not on the mind the sky clouds   38
When The Sun Leaps Tremendous   42
When the sun leaps tremendous from the rim   42
When tobacco came, when Raleigh did first bring   26
When tobacco came, when Raleigh first did bring   29
Who would have thought the men that watched the stars   74
Wonderful falls makes Cotswold edge, it drops   50
Wraith of grey cloud in Leckhampton elbow   28